*f*P

ALSO BY MARCUS BUCKINGHAM

First, Break All the Rules
Now, Discover Your Strengths
The One Thing You Need to Know

GO

PUT YOUR STRENGTHS TO WORK

6 POWERFUL STEPS TO ACHIEVE OUTSTANDING PERFORMANCE

MARCUS BUCKINGHAM

Free Press

New York London Toronto Sydney

*f*P

FREE PRESS
A Division of Simon & Schuster, Inc.
1230 Avenue of the Americas
New York, NY 10020

For information regarding special discounts for bulk purchases,
please contact Simon & Schuster Special Sales at 1-800-456-6798
or business@simonandschuster.com

Designed by Nancy Singer Olaguera

Manufactured in the United States of America

3   5   7   9   10   8   6   4   2

Library of Congress Cataloging-in-Publication Data is available.

ISBN-13: 978-0-7432-6167-8
ISBN-10:   0-7432-6167-4

To Janie, Jack, and Lilia:
We are all in this one together.

step 1	**BUST THE MYTHS** So, What's Stopping You?
step 2	**GET CLEAR** Do You Know What Your Strengths Are?
step 3	**FREE YOUR STRENGTHS** How Do You Make the Most of What Strengthens You?
step 4	**STOP YOUR WEAKNESSES** How Can You Cut Out What Weakens You?
step 5	**SPEAK UP** How Do You Create Strong Teams?
step 6	**BUILD STRONG HABITS** How Can You Make This Last Forever?

CONTENTS

GO

PUT YOUR
STRENGTHS
TO WORK

INTRODUCTION

LEAD THIS MOVEMENT

THE FIRST STAGE: HOW TO LABEL

It's hard to trace the source of the strengths movement.

Some will identify Peter Drucker, citing his seminal 1966 book, *The Effective Executive,* in which he wrote: "The effective executive builds on strengths—their own strengths, the strengths of superiors, colleagues, subordinates; and on the strengths of the situation."

Some will cite a 1987 article that launched a new discipline called Appreciative Inquiry, whose basic premise, according to its founder, David Cooperrider, was "to build organizations around what works rather than fix what doesn't."

Some will make reference to Dr. Martin Seligman's 1999 speech after becoming president of the American Psychological Association. "The most important thing we learned was that psychology was half-baked, literally half-baked," he said. "We've baked the part about mental illness, about repair of damage. The other side's unbaked, the side of strength, the side of what we're good at."

More recently, some might even point to the book I wrote with Donald Clifton for the Gallup organization, *Now, Discover Your Strengths,* which began with this optimistic statement of intent: "We wrote this book to start a revolution, the strengths revolution."

Whatever its true source, the strengths movement is now in full flood. It is a wave of change that, over the last several years, has swept us all forward. No discipline has been left behind. Whether we work in business, government, education, or health care, this wave has lifted us up, spun us around, and revealed to us all a new world. You may not yet recognize the change—some of us were bowled over by the wave, while others barely noticed it carrying them along. But, with or without our knowledge, it has picked us up and deposited us far from where we were a decade ago. And there's no going back. This wave has forever changed the way we perceive ourselves, our employees, our students, and our children.

Look around you, and you'll see clearly the signs of change.

Many of the world's most successful organizations such as Wells Fargo, Intel, Best Buy, and Accenture have declared their commitment to becoming an explicitly strengths-based organization. All new managers at Toyota must now attend a three-day Great Manager training program that shows them how to spot the strengths of their subordinates. All new managers at Yahoo are required to take an online survey that measures their talents and pinpoints their strongest.

Look beyond business, and you'll see nonprofit organizations such as the U.S. Coast Guard, the Baptist General Convention of Oklahoma, the American Society on Aging, and the New Zealand Ministry of Youth Development all installing similar strengths-based programs and initiatives.

Universities too have been swept up by the movement. Princeton, with great fanfare, recently set up its own Center for Health and Well-Being, dedicated to the study of all that is right in the world. Over half the faculty are, surprisingly, economists. At Harvard, Professor Tal David Ben-Shahar's class An Introduction to Positive Psychology is now the most popular elective class in the entire curriculum. And Azusa Pacific University now has a Center for Strengths-Based Education, set up by the pioneering educator Edward "Chip" Anderson.

Look further still, and you'll see more signs of the movement's reach. If your child happens to break the law in Ingham County, Michigan, before his day in probate court, he'll be asked to fill out a Strengths Assessment for Juvenile Justice, which will pose strengths-based questions such as "Have you made any good changes in the past? How did you make these changes?" and "What is your first step to get out of this trouble? Who will be the first person to notice this step?"

If you are a psychiatry student learning to work with patients suffering persistent mental disorders, you will be asked to read Charles Rapp's 1997 classic, *The Strengths Model*, which shows you, case by case, how to "amplify the well part of the patient."

If you are an aspiring soccer coach, Major League Soccer will be happy to sign you up for its Strengths-Based Coaching course. Here you'll learn, among other things, how to hand out "green cards," which draw a child's attention to a particularly good pass or tackle he made, rather than the traditionally puni-tive yellow and red cards.

Today the strengths movement is everywhere: the corporate world, the worlds of public service, of economics, of education, of faith, of charity—it has affected them all. It has its detractors, of course, but an appeal as universal as this begs the question "Why?" Why do so many people from so many different worlds see such power in the strengths-based perspective?

Because it works better than any other perspective. The radical idea at the core of the strengths movement is that excel-lence is not the opposite of failure, and that, as such, you will learn little about excellence from studying failure. This seems like an obvious idea until you realize that, before the strengths movement began, virtually all business and academic inquiry was built on the opposite idea: namely, that a deep understand-ing of failure leads to an equally deep understanding of excel-lence. That's why we studied unhappy customers to learn about the happy ones, employees' weaknesses to learn how to make them excel, sickness to learn about health, divorce to learn about marriage, and sadness to learn about joy.

What has become evident in virtually every field of human endeavor is that failure and success are not opposites, they are merely different, and so they must be studied separately. Thus, for example, if you want to learn what you should *not* do after an environmental disaster, Chernobyl will be instructive. But if you want to learn what you *should* do, Chernobyl is a waste. Only successful cleanups, such as at the Rocky Flats nuclear facility in Colorado, can tell you what excellence looks like.

Study unproductive teams, and you soon discover that the teammates argue a lot. Study successful teams, and you learn that they argue just as much. To find the secrets to a great team, you have to investigate the successful ones and figure out what is going on in the space between the arguments.

Focus your research on people who contract HIV and die, and you gain some useful insights about how the disease wrecks the body's immune system. But focus your research on those few people with HIV who are relatively unaffected by the disease, and you learn something else entirely: namely, how the body fights back.

Conventional wisdom tells us that we learn from our mistakes. The strengths movement says that all we learn from mistakes are the characteristics of mistakes. If we want to learn about our successes, we must study successes.

Fueled by this idea, the first stage of the strengths movement—the stage we are in right now—has been dominated by efforts to label what is right with things. Thus, whereas the World Bank used to rank countries according to their negative qualities, such as poverty, violence, and vulnerability, today it has developed a list of positive labels that capture a country's overall level of well-being, labels such as social capability, economic self-determination, and sustainability of local customs.

In the field of psychology, our descriptors all used to be heavily skewed toward the negatives: neurotic, psychotic, schizophrenic, depressed. Today we have redressed the balance and have added equally detailed labels to describe the positives. For example, Martin Seligman and his colleague Chris Peterson have developed their list of "Character Strengths and Virtues," which includes such qualities as Courage, Justice, Transcendence, and Temperance.

Similarly, *Now, Discover Your Strengths* introduced Gallup's online personality profile called StrengthsFinder (since renamed the Clifton StrengthsFinder, in Don's memory), which measures you on thirty-four themes of talent, with names like Ideation, Restorative, Significance, and Connectedness.

Our hunger for these labels can be measured in part by the number of people who have taken the Clifton StrengthsFinder profile since 2001. The total is now over two million. More revealing still, each year this number not only increases, but the *increase* increases. More people took it last year than the year before, and more the year before than the year before that. Clearly, millions of us feel a deep need to label what's right with us.

THE SECOND STAGE: HOW TO TAKE ACTION

If all this labeling is to not go to waste, however, we must now take the necessary next step. We must progress into the second stage of the strengths movement: the action stage. This is where we learn how to go beyond the affirming power of a label. It's the stage where we engage with the real world, where we figure out how to use our strengths to make a tangible contribution, where we deal with people who don't agree on what our strengths are, or who don't care, or who do care but want us to focus them differently than we do. It's the stage where we step up and put our strengths to work.

This book leads us into the second stage, where the real payoff is to be found.

While the labeling stage was driven by the theoretical idea that you learn little about excellence from studying failure, the action stage is founded on a more pragmatic premise: namely, that a person or an organization will excel only by amplifying strengths, never by simply fixing weaknesses.

At the level of the organization, this premise has been both widely disseminated and well executed. Drawing on the economic theories of the eighteenth-century economist David Riccardo, Peter Drucker wrote that the most competitive companies, just like the most competitive countries, "get their strengths together and make their weaknesses irrelevant." Jim Collins in his book *Good to Great* captured the same idea when he wrote that great companies focus on those few things they can be "the best in the world at." Study any effective organization, from Starbucks to Lexus, Apple to Dell, Wal-Mart to Best Buy, and you will see that many have figured out how to put this advice into practice.

At the level of the individual, this idea has been equally widely disseminated. The second page of *Now, Discover Your Strengths* references a study of 198,000 employees from thirty-six companies who were asked whether they had the chance to play to their strengths every day. Those who strongly agreed that they did "were 50 percent more likely to work in teams with lower employee turnover, 38 percent more likely to work in more productive teams, and 44 percent more likely to work in teams with higher customer satisfaction scores. And over time, those teams that increased the number of employees who strongly agreed saw comparable increases in productivity, customer loyalty, and employee retention." Today there are now many further studies confirming and extending these findings, the most comprehensive of which is the study of more than 8,000 teams by Jim Harter and Frank Schmidt, published in the *Journal of Applied Psychology.*

The conclusion to be drawn from all these studies is clear: While there are many good levers for engaging people and driving performance—levers such as selecting for talent, setting clear expectations, praising where praise is due, and defining the team's mission—the *master lever* is getting each person to play to his strengths. Pull this lever, and an engaged and productive team will be the result. Fail to pull it, and no matter what else is done to motivate the team, it'll never fully engage. It will never become a high-performance team.

And organizations pay homage to these studies when they say "Our people are our greatest asset." Though, in truth, they don't actually mean this. What they mean is "Our people's *strengths* are our greatest asset." After all, organizations place a premium on their employees because in today's knowledge and service economy, the value of the employees lies in their creativity, innovation, and good judgment. None of us, though, is creative, or innovative, or has good judgment in every single aspect of our work. On the contrary, each of us has some aspects of our work where we aren't very creative at all, where our first idea is not only our best idea, it's our only idea. We keep talking, but there's nothing there; the well is dry. By contrast, each of us is at our most creative, our most innovative, and shows our best judgment precisely in our areas of greatest strength. You don't focus on people's strengths to make them happier. You do it to make them better performers. What these studies reveal is that no matter what the team, no matter what the organization, when you do, they are. That's why the best organizations are now so public in their commitment to become strengths based.

Despite the loud support for this idea, however, the evidence reveals that most of us still don't know how to do it. In fact, the evidence is even more damning than that. It shows that even though we now know how to put a label on our strengths, we still have little idea how to take control of our work and steer it toward these strengths. Back in 2001, polls revealed that only 20 percent of us claimed to be able to put our strengths to work every day. Today, despite more than two million people taking the Clifton StrengthsFinder profile, when you poll people with the question "What percentage of a typical day do you spend playing to your strengths?" only 17 percent answer "most of the time."

Now, I'm not a Pollyanna. I didn't expect 80 percent of people to say that they have the chance to play to their strengths most of the time. Our time is not our own, as we are pulled in different directions by our colleagues, our customers, and our organization's shifting expectations.

Still, 17 percent? This number seems wastefully low. Let's say, in a bow to the challenges of the real world, we're granted fully a quarter of our typical day to fill with those annoying non-negotiables we all have in our job. We can have 25 percent of our day—from the time we arrive through eleven in the morning, each and every morning—to fill with the calls we don't like making, the emails that drag us down, the mundane reports that refuse to write themselves, the grumpy guy down the hall who daily insists on barging into our office and unloading his problems on us. Twenty-five percent of every day bequeathed to activities that bore us or frustrate us or just leave us cold.

All right, but this still leaves vast stretches of time, 75 percent of our time, that could be filled with activities that call upon some aspect of our strengths. What these data reveal is that only

17 percent of us have managed to fill this time with activities such as these. Only 17 percent of us have our strengths in play most of the time. The truth is, we are not our organization's greatest asset, at least not nearly to the extent that we could be.

When it comes to the strengths movement, we are stuck in the first stage. We know how to label. We don't know how to move beyond a label and actually put our strengths to work. If the subject were physical strengths rather than psychological, it's as if we know how to measure the different elements of fitness—weight, heart rate, good cholesterol, body fat—but not how to exercise. And so, although we know a great deal more than we did before the strengths movement began, we're still not getting any fitter.

This book is about how to exercise. It's about how to get unstuck and step confidently into the second stage. It's about how to identify what is best and most effective in you and then apply it in the real world. It's not a book of theory. It's a practical book, one that teaches you a powerful new discipline. Learn this discipline, practice it each week, and you will soon find yourself able to take control and unleash fully the force of your strengths. Whatever potential your strengths possess, the world will come to see them, and your performance, your career, and the significance of your contribution will be forever changed.

I recently presented the 17 percent figure to a group of chief executives and finished my talk by saying that, as yet, large organizations have proven themselves to be an inefficient mechanism for getting the most out of each employee. At which point, one of them started laughing. "Do you really think," he said, "that in my position *I* can carve a role for myself where I really get to play to my strengths most of the time? Come on, I've got far too many responsibilities to be able to do that."

He does indeed have lots of responsibilities. He also has

a ton of discretion. He of all people should be able to take control of his time at work and gradually steer it toward his strengths and away from his weaknesses. If the newest frontline employee struggles to fill his days with activities that call upon his strengths, well, he has our understanding and our sympathy. He's not off the hook, by any means, but we can certainly see why he might feel a little constrained by his circumstances.

The chief executive, on the other hand, has no such constraints. If he laughs at the notion that it's his responsibility to figure out how to put his strengths into play each and every day, then perhaps it's little wonder that so few of the rest of us manage it.

And yet clearly it *is* possible. A little less than two out of ten people succeed in capitalizing on their strengths, but at least there are those two. And, as the research reveals, those two are significantly more productive, more customer focused, and more likely to stick around than the rest of us. So, for large organizations, once they've figured out how to get the chief executive to stop laughing, the profitable question to ask is "How can we build the kind of workplace where more than two out of ten people use their strengths for most of the day?"

That is an important question, one that deserves a great deal more focus than it's getting, but it's not the question that this book deals with. No, this book asks "Are you one of the two out of ten? And if you're not, how do you get to be?"

YOU ARE HERE

To answer the first question definitively, take the Strengths Engagement Track, or SET. This short survey has proven to be the best way to measure how engaged a person's strengths are, and, when combined, how engaged an entire team's strengths are.

To reveal your score, take the jacket off your book and look on the inside of the jacket. You will find an ID code. Log onto www.SimplyStrengths.com, enter your code, and answer the questions. You will immediately see your individual results displayed like this:

The top dial is the Present dial. It reveals how engaged your strengths are currently, as compared to a nationally representative sample of the working population of the United States. Thus, if your needle is pointing to the number 50, you are in the 50th percentile; if it points to the number 74, you are in the 74th percentile, and so on.

Whatever your score is, think of it as a measure of how well you are doing at living up to your potential. If you score 62, and a colleague of yours scores 74, this doesn't mean that she is necessarily more productive than you are—though she may be. It simply reveals that, currently, she is engaging her strengths more consistently than you are and therefore is expressing more of her strengths' potential.

If you are a manager, you should have your entire team take the survey to see how much of your team's strengths' potential is being used. To do this, after you and your team have entered your ID codes from the dust jacket of the book and have taken the SET survey, follow the directions on SimplyStrengths.com to link each of your team members' scores together to create an overall team score. You'll immediately see which percentile your team is in.

The bottom dial is the Future dial. It reveals how engaged your strengths, or your team's strengths, are going to be. It represents your trend line. Thus, if you score low on this dial, as in the example, this strongly suggests that, whatever your Present score is, it is likely to decrease. If you score high on this Future dial, the likelihood is that your Present score will go up.

The survey captures this by asking a few questions about your mind-set and your behaviors. Thus, if your Future dial is low, this means that your mind-set and your behaviors are not consistent with the discipline of putting your strengths to work. Your strengths may be engaged in the present, but because you didn't engage them by thinking right and acting right—your mind-set and your actions were off the mark—the chances are slim that your current level of engagement will last. Right now your strengths may be engaged, but it's because of something your manager did, or because of who your teammates happen to be, or because of pure good fortune. The slightest change in your environment, however—a new boss, a new client, a reorganization of your department—and your strengths will likely disengage.

Of course, top performing teams and individuals score high on both dials. Their strengths are engaged, and because they know why and how, they are likely to sustain these levels of engagement no matter what the world throws at them. The goal of this book is to equip you with the insights and the routines to drive both dials, so that you can engage your strengths right now and then make this engagement last.

So take the survey. Read the rest of the book. Do the activities suggested along the way. Then retake the survey when you finish the book. The dials will move, and so will your performance.

AND YOU'RE CLOSER THAN YOU THINK

Conventional wisdom tells us that our ideal job is far removed from our present situation, "out there" somewhere in a mythic world where we are our own boss, telecommuting from our cabin in the hills, doing what we love, making loads of money along the way, disturbed only by the whinnying of our horse and the scent of the wet trees.

Tempting though this mental picture is, the data don't support it. Ask a nationally representative sample of the workforce what their ideal job is, and 60 percent of them say either "what I'm doing now, with increased responsibility" or "a specialized subset of what I'm doing now." Only 31 percent say "a different job."

Ask them why they took their current job, and the most common answer is "greater opportunity to do more of what I like to do." "More money" comes in second.

Ask them how often they feel an emotional high at work—a sure sign that they're playing to a strength—and 51 percent say "about once a week."

Ask them how often they get so involved in what they are doing at work that they lose track of time—another strength-in-play sign—and 73 percent say "about once a week."

Yes, there are a few of us who are massively miscast—accountants who want to be astronauts, engineers who yearn to be entrepreneurs—but most of us aren't. Most of us have heard the voice of our strengths loudly enough to seek out roles that call upon some aspect of our strengths at least once a week. Most of us are in the vicinity.

But we can't win on once a week. We can't make our greatest and longest-lasting contribution on once a week. We can't achieve anything of any significance on once a week. In fact, no matter how noble our sense of mission is, or how cool our company is, or how supportive our teammates are, most of us burn out on once a week.

So our challenge now is to increase dramatically how often we play to our strengths. On high-performance teams, people say they call upon their strengths more than 75 percent of the time. For us to reach this level, we don't need to cast aside our current work and strike out for the perfect dream job. Besides, that perfect job doesn't exist. Confucius said, "Find a job you love, and you'll never work a day in your life," but this is one of those few occasions where we'd be wise to ignore him. None of us, no matter how content we are at work, loves our entire job. Whatever our job happens to be, it doesn't consist of one activity. It comprises many different activities. Some invigorate us, some leave us neutral, and some deplete us, or bore us, or drain us. Given this, holding out for that perfect "job we love" is a fool's game.

Instead, we simply need to learn how to take our existing job and each week, reshape it around our strengths—even in the face of interference from the world around us. To do this, we need to master a new discipline, one that brings order and focus to a series of incremental moves. Put this discipline into practice each week, and we will gradually, degree by degree, tilt the playing field so that the *best* of our job becomes *most* of our job.

In sequential order: First, we need to sort through our activities and pinpoint precisely which ones invigorate us and which deplete us. Second, while others are pulling us in every direction, we need to stay sufficiently in control of our hours at work so that, over time, we load up on the invigorating kind and push back hard if the scales gradually tip the other way. Third, we must learn how to explain what we are doing persuasively enough to get our colleagues to want to help us. And fourth, whenever we get a new boss or a new job or a new corporate directive, we must stay clearheaded enough to keep our weeks intentionally tilted toward the invigorating activities and away from the others.

Simply put, we need to ditch the typical "pull" approach to work and replace it with the "push" discipline.

"Pull" looks like this: Somebody else tells you what is expected of you. You listen carefully, and then, in the language of these expectations, your goals are set for you. Your best hope for achievement and reward, you tell yourself, is to try to focus your time so that you spend most of it on those few activities that will really drive your goals. As such, your goals pull you toward certain activities and away from others.

The "push" discipline looks very different. It begins with you taking responsibility for identifying your own strengths and weaknesses—as you'll see later, no one can do this better than you. Then, having identified them, you take a stand for them. In practical terms, this means that you push the people at work, along with their many expectations, toward your strengths and away from your weaknesses. These people—your colleagues, your customers, your manager—are good people, with good and appropriate expectations of you, but they don't know your strengths. Which means that they don't know where you will be at your most productive, or where you will come up with your best ideas, or where you will spontaneously set challenging goals for yourself, or where your inquisitiveness will stay sparked, or where you will reach down willingly for that extra ounce of effort when things don't go your way. They don't know any of these things about you.

But you do. So if they want to see all of these qualities from you at work, and they surely do, then it's your responsibility to know how to push each week for more opportunities to play to your strengths. Push for more training around your strengths. Push for inclusion on teams or projects that could really use your strengths. Push to spend time with colleagues who share one of your strengths and are even more adept than you at applying it. And, of course, push away, as far as you can and as quickly as you can, those activities that call upon your weaknesses.

This doesn't mean you should swagger into work each day and demand that you be asked to do only strength-based activities. No one would want to work with you if you did this. But what you can do each week, late on a Friday evening or early on a Monday morning, is start this new discipline. A discipline that begins with the simple question "How will I ensure that I put my strengths into play just a little more this week than I did last week?" and ends with your building your job around the best of you.

If you're a manager, this sounds radical, but, in fact, this is exactly what you want your employees to be doing. You want them to be pushing you to load up on their strengths. Why? Because you want them to be both productive today and resilient tomorrow. You want them to be creative, come up with new ideas, and seize the initiative. In corporate speak, you want them to take responsibility for their own performance and development.

The hard thing is that, as managers, though we find ourselves saying these words, we are frequently frustrated when our people don't step up and do it. But don't blame your people. They do indeed want to contribute, to showcase their best, and to push themselves to develop their strengths. They do want to step up. But faced with a world that is ambivalent about their strengths—supportive when a strength helps get the job done, dismissive when it doesn't—they just don't know how.

This book will help them. It will instill in them a lifelong, six-step discipline for putting their strengths to work.

However, you can't transform your team, your colleagues, your division, or your entire organization until you know how to transform your own performance at work. As the airlines would say, you need to put on your own oxygen mask before you start trying to help those around you. So before you hand the book off to your employees, read it for yourself. Learn to master the discipline. Take the required steps. Become expert at putting your own strengths to work.

Only then teach others what you've learned.

THE 6-STEP DISCIPLINE

Here, in a brief overview, are the six steps that make up this discipline:

Step 1. Bust the Myths

You will succeed in putting your strengths to work only if you believe that capitalizing on your strengths is the best way to compete. Many organizations now do. Most individuals still don't. Ask people point-blank "Is finding your weaknesses and fixing them the best way to achieve outstanding performance?" and, in repeated polls, 87 percent either agree or strongly agree.

If you count yourself in this overwhelming majority, you are going to have a hard time persevering through the remaining steps. So in the first step, you'll confront the three myths that keep so many of us locked in this remedial mind-set, and bust them.

Step 2. Get Clear

Armed with a strengths-based mind-set, you'll take the next step: identifying your own strengths and weaknesses. And by strengths and weaknesses, I'm not referring to a list of personality labels such as those you might learn if you took the Clifton StrengthsFinder, or Myers-Briggs Type Indicator (MBTI), or the Kolbe Conative Index, or DiSC, or any similar personality profile.

These kinds of profiles ask you to respond to various questions or pairs of descriptive statements. Then they collate your answers and present you with a summary of your strongest patterns of thought, feeling, or behavior. For example, my top two patterns as identified by the Clifton StrengthsFinder are Futuristic and Context. Futuristic tells me that I am the kind of person who enjoys projecting into the future and seeing images in my head of how much better things could be. Context reveals that I tend to be uncomfortable until I understand which factors combined to create the current situation I'm facing or how a particular person came to be who he is. In short, I love to look forward but need to look back before I can indulge this love. Or, less generously, since I am fascinated by both the future and the past, I quite often find myself missing out on the present.

These kinds of insights are intriguing to me and to others who need to deal with me, but, to be clear, neither Futuristic nor Context are strengths of mine. They are merely patterns, predispositions to see and engage with the world in a particular way. They can offer a signpost toward my strengths, but they are not my strengths. My strengths, as defined in *Now, Discover Your Strengths,* can be found in those activities in which I exhibit "consistent, near-perfect performance." My strengths are those *specific activities* at which I do well and for which I still retain a powerful appetite. (I'll describe a couple of my specific strengths later in step two.)

So are yours. If you are going to join the two out of ten, if you are going to succeed in pushing your time toward your strengths, you must learn how to go beyond the labels of any personality test that you may have taken and identify the specific, real-world activities that constitute your strengths.

With the right techniques, this isn't so hard to do. In step two you'll learn how. You'll learn whether your strengths are best defined as "what you're good at" or "what you love to do." You'll learn who the best judge of your strengths is, you or the people around you. And most important, you'll learn how to sift through the mudslide of activities, responsibilities, and relationships that each week comes down upon you, and get clear on which are strengths and which are weaknesses.

Step 3. Free Your Strengths

When we ask people why they don't get to play to their strengths at work, the most common first reaction is a look of bemused resignation. They'll say things like "The world isn't made for my happiness," or "There's a reason they call it 'work,'" or "Mine isn't the kind of job where you can really do that," and then go on to contrast their job with journalism or acting or teaching, which supposedly are the kind where you can.

It's as though they've long ago given up the belief that work will be a place in which they will get to express their strengths. If anything, the pendulum has, over the years, swung far in the other direction, leaving them suspicious of their strengths at work and mindful of the need to keep them on a tight leash.

Of course, it wasn't always this way, was it? You weren't always so distanced from your strengths. Back when you were young, your strengths were to be trusted. You might not have had a name for them—you might not have even labeled them strengths—but when you were a child, you listened to them. You knew which activities drew you back time and again. You knew which situations thrilled you, and you sought them out. You knew which kids you wanted to hang out with, and, in the same vein, you knew not only which subjects interested you, but which teachers you really wanted teaching those subjects. You knew this when you got out of bed every morning, and you had faith in this certainty. You felt your yearnings and your passions intensely, and they fueled your innocent belief that the world was going to wait for you, until one day you would emerge from your home or your school, and you would get to make your unique mark on the world.

How old were you when you still felt this? Eight? Ten?

And then somehow, sometime between then and now, your childish clarity faded, and you started listening to the world around you more closely than you did to yourself. The world was persuasive and loud, and so you resigned yourself to conforming to its demands. You had to get into college, study what your parents and teachers advised you to study. You had to get a job and pay the bills and pay off those loans. And then you got the job, and with the job came a job description and a performance appraisal and a career ladder and a set of customers—and, to manage all this for you, a boss. In the midst of all these expectations, your strengths became, if not irrelevant, then merely a curiosity, to be touched on briefly during your annual review before the serious business of your performance and your development needs and your career were discussed.

And so today, when you're asked why you aren't one of the two out of ten, you look around and point to the world and say, in effect, "How could I be? My manager and my teammates have a long list of things they worry about at work, and giving me the chance to play to my strengths isn't necessarily one of them."

And you'd be right. Most conversations at work do not concern your strengths. We asked a representative sample of the American workforce this question: "When you and your manager discuss your performance, what do you spend the most time talking about, strengths or weaknesses?" Thirty-five percent of the respondents said weaknesses: forty percent said, "My manager doesn't talk to me about these things." Only twenty-five percent said strengths.

So yes, you'd be right that your world at work isn't much concerned with you and your strengths. But so what? Faced with this kind of indifference from the world around you, you've got two choices: either resign yourself to a life in which your strengths, whatever they may be, are largely irrelevant, or learn how to make them relevant.

In step three, you'll learn how to do the latter. You'll learn the different strategies for volunteering your strengths to the team, and you'll become handy with two tools: one that helps you to generate ideas about how your strengths can help the team, and another that puts these ideas into practice.

Step 4. Stop Your Weaknesses

You'll fall off your strengths path quickly if you don't know how to navigate away from those activities that weaken you. For many reasons, this proves especially challenging. First, because it takes a fair amount of creativity to figure out how to stop doing what weakens you yet still get your job done.

Second, because, even if you generate some good ideas, it's hard not to feel guilty or self-absorbed when you start to put these ideas into practice. The world at large reserves a special kind of praise for those of us who suffer through it, who keep at it no matter what. In the face of this, to stop focusing on a weakness can feel a lot like giving up, or handing off.

And, third, because, as the data reveal, most of us don't think we should steer away from our weaknesses. On the contrary, 87 percent of us believe that we should take dead aim at our weaknesses and work diligently to improve them.

So bring all of your resolve to step four. What you'll learn here is the mirror image of what you learned in step three: the best strategies for lessening the impact of your weaknesses on the team, and the tools both to generate ideas and apply these ideas in the real world.

Step 5. Speak Up

When was the last time you talked with someone about your strengths and weaknesses? What were you trying to communicate? How did it go? Did you achieve what you wanted to achieve?

At work, the two most common situations where you should have a my-strengths-and-weaknesses conversation are the how-are-we-going-to-divide-up-the-work conversation with your teammates, and, the one-on-one with your manager.

Although these two situations have their own dynamic, in both you are trying to communicate the same thing: "Listen, there are certain activities that thrill me and challenge me, and others that seem to bore me or drain me. I am going to contribute my utmost if I spend more time on the first kind and less on the other kind. Can you help?"

You're not trying to pull the wool over anyone's eyes. You're not trying to make life easy for you and difficult for everyone else. You're not trying to get out of working hard. You just want them to know where your shoulders are broadest, where they can expect the most from you, and, on the flip side, where they need to tread a little lightly. And you don't want them to know this because you're some sensitive little flower who needs special treatment or otherwise you'll crumple. You simply want them to know how to set you up so that you can make your greatest possible contribution. If everything went perfectly, that is what your listeners would take away from each of these conversations.

That doesn't happen very often.

When you talk with your teammates, deep down, you may genuinely want them to learn about your strengths and weaknesses so that they can know where you can be counted on to help them the most, but somehow it doesn't come across this way. Most people think (and you may be one of them) that everyone views the array of activities at work in pretty much the same light. There are "good" activities, which everyone would love to do. And "rotten" activities, which no one would. Your conversations with teammates thus tend to be colored by the unspoken premise that you are trying to load up on the good ones while surreptitiously handing off the rotten ones to them. Or, if your relationships are more trusting than this, your conversation becomes a friendly negotiation about how you and they can share equal portions of good and rotten activities.

Either way, it's a rare day when you end one of these conversations knowing in detail about one another's strengths and weaknesses and how you can complement one another.

This kind of miscommunication reaches its height during those one-on-ones with your manager. Ideally, this conversation would be a free exchange of ideas about how you could steer your week toward your strengths and away from your weaknesses. This would demand a fair degree of creativity from both of you, since it isn't always immediately obvious (or possible) how you can sculpt the work to fit you. But, in this ideal world, you would at least be having this conversation.

In the real world, however, you don't. You may hope to be, and your manager may even begin the one-on-one saying that sculpting your work to fit you is indeed the purpose of it, but you and she both know that it isn't. You both recognize that there are other agendas at play governing what you say. And so as you sit facing each other, you choose your words very carefully.

You're thinking: "How can I get out of this conversation with as much approval as possible, yet still get what I want in terms of pay and career opportunities?"

You're thinking: "If I claim to be strong at something, she may seize on this as a chance to set her expectations even higher. Or she may put a label on me, and come to see me as having *only* this one strength, and then load me up with additional responsibilities that I may not like or want."

You're thinking: "I can't honestly tell her what my weaknesses are. She'll think I'm complaining. Or she'll tell me that she couldn't agree more and that this year I should really work on improving them."

The upshot is that you aren't as candid as you should be or could be. Instead you dance around each other, never quite getting to the heart of who you are and how you can make the greatest contribution possible—which is, ironically, what you both want.

If you are going to sustain your highest possible level of performance, you're going to have to learn how to excel at each of these conversations. You need to master the art of talking about your strengths without bragging and your weaknesses without whining.

In step five you'll learn how.

Step 6. Build Strong Habits

Most of us have been one of the two out of ten at some point in our career. By accident, by force of will, or by the grace of a good boss, we have found ourselves in a position where we're playing to our strengths the grand majority of the time. And while it lasts, it's a special feeling: When we're not working, we find ourselves actually looking forward to going to work. When we are working, we feel challenged in just the way we like to be challenged, simultaneously in our zone yet pushed a little beyond it; in control but not entirely comfortable. And when we leave, we feel authentic, fulfilled, valued.

Sure, even during these times, our work still has moments of frustration and drudgery and disappointment, but these moments are a tiny minority. The overarching feeling we have is that work is a wonderful place where we get to express how truly effective and powerful we can be.

The Greeks coined a term to describe this feeling. They called it *eudaimonia,* which translates as the feeling "of giving your best where you have the best to give, and of reaping the rewards of this excellence"—or more simply, and in all senses of the word, the feeling of flourishing. So, yes, at these times work can be wonderful because at work we can flourish.

Then something changes. Sometimes the change is obviously negative, such as an annoying new boss or a companywide downsizing. Sometimes it is superficially positive—we are offered an exciting new promotion or the chance to participate on a high-profile project team. Sometimes the change is sudden—we're fired. Sometimes it's imperceptible—a client slowly grows, and its requests of us shift and morph.

However it occurs, this change fills our weeks with different activities. Some continue to call upon our strengths, but many do not. If we are not especially vigilant, we find that we are carried along by these new activities; they take up more of our time, demand more of our attention, and, after a while, we wake up and discover that we have veered far off our strengths path.

To keep on it for our entire career, we need to stay clear-headed. We need to build the right habits, so that week in, week out, and year upon year, we stay in control, always pushing toward activities that strengthen us, ever watchful for those that drag us down.

Step six, the last step, shows you how.

Here again is the chart showing the sequence of steps you will follow.

step 1	**BUST THE MYTHS** So, What's Stopping You?

step 2	**GET CLEAR** Do You Know What Your Strengths Are?

step 3	**FREE YOUR STRENGTHS** How Do You Make the Most of What Strengthens You?

step 4	**STOP YOUR WEAKNESSES** How Can You Cut Out What Weakens You?

step 5	**SPEAK UP** How Do You Create Strong Teams?

step 6	**BUILD STRONG HABITS** How Can You Make This Last Forever?

• • •

Throughout the book, we'll be asking you to put your learnings into practice immediately. Your success in becoming one of the two out of ten depends largely on the specifics of your strengths and weaknesses, your situation at work, and the people you work with. The steps in the book can give you a way of looking at your life at work, a set of routines to follow, and practical tips for putting these routines into practice, but it'll be up to you to fine-tune them. You'll have to try them out, to use the realities of your working life to tweak them, and then bring your discoveries back to the discipline as you read on.

Indeed, the steps comprise a choreographed sequence of activities. Step two works best only if you've done the work at the end of step one. Step three requires you to have tried out the activities at the end of step two, and so on throughout the book.

These activities will not take you away from your work. You'll find no role-playing, no theoretical exercises. Instead we'll ask you to focus on your work as never before, not only because you don't have the time to get pulled away from your work, but more importantly because you'll use your existing work as the raw material for discovering what your strengths and weaknesses are, and for learning how to push your time toward the former and away from the latter. Since your challenges lie in the actual activities with which you've filled your week, the solutions must lie there also.

So what you have in this book is a six-week, six-step discipline. Each step constitutes a week of reading, action, and learning, and each week builds on the one before. We don't suggest you sit down and try to read the book in one sitting—you won't have time to do the activities, so you won't learn what you need to learn. Instead, read one step per week, and during the week, do the relevant activities. Stay on track as closely as you can, week by week, and try to resist the temptation to jump ahead. The book will prove most helpful when you stick to this weekly rhythm of read, act, learn.

Keep up this rhythm, and, by the end of the book, you'll know how to take a stand for your strengths and leverage them as never before. Your performance will soar, and more significant still, you'll know how to sustain this level of performance throughout the many twists and turns of your career.

TROMBONE PLAYER WANTED

To start you off, watch step one of *Trombone Player Wanted*. This is a fourteen-minute short film that brings the strengths movement to life. It captures why the movement is so important, presents the three myths that are holding it back, and describes why we must replace these myths with three new, strengths-based truths.

To access it, log onto SimplyStrengths.com, enter your code from the book jacket, and you will be able to download the entire first film. This first film of the *Trombone Player Wanted* series can stand by itself. In writing it, we wanted to take you back to when you were nine or ten, the last time the sound of your strengths inside your head was louder and clearer than the demands of the world at large. So the story introduces you to a boy, Ewan, who wants to find . . . well, he wants to find a trombone player.

You'll notice that this film is actually the first in a series of six short films, where each film corresponds to the same numbered step in this book. Thus the first film challenges you to BUST THE MYTHS, the second helps you GET CLEAR on what your strengths are, the third addresses how to FREE YOUR STRENGTHS, and so on.

Because each film covers the same ground as the corresponding step, you don't need to watch the films in order to get the most out of the book. But if you're the kind of person who is energized by images and character and story, you may want to purchase all of them. (The book jacket code enables one download of the first two films for free.)

Above all, as you read the book or watch the films, know that you have much more room to maneuver than you might think. To build your life around your strengths, you don't need to wait for the perfect job, the perfect boss, or the perfect situation. Besides, these things may never come. Instead learn how to take stock of your strengths, how to take control of your time, and how to make the two gradually, inexorably, and deliberately converge.

Start with your own life, and to paraphrase Mahatma Gandhi, be the change you want to see in your team.

Lead this movement.

STEP 1

BUST THE MYTHS

"SO, WHAT'S STOPPING YOU?"

MEET HEIDI

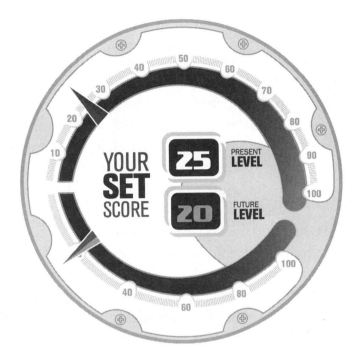

Above you'll see Heidi's SET score when she began the six-week discipline. You should get to know Heidi because, although she is an actual person, her experiences speak to everyman and everywoman.

On the surface, her situation is unremarkable. She works hard in the anonymous middle ranks of a large, effective, and unglamorous organization.

Look closer, though, and pay attention to the specifics. Her organization, Hampton hotels, although situated toward the midscale end of the hospitality spectrum, is a truly great company. Its fourteen hundred hotels, all run by franchisees, serve as the standard for the industry. When Marriott decided to enter this market with Courtyard and Fairfield Inn, its stated goal was to mirror the quality and efficiency of Hampton hotels. The company is very successful financially. It is also an obsessively guest-focused company, driven by its 100 percent Hampton Satisfaction Guarantee "If you're not 100% satisfied, we don't expect you to pay."

Heidi was not just marking time in this great company. She was (and still is) a top-notch brand director for Hampton hotels. Her job was to ensure that her region of hotels conformed to the rigorous brand standards laid out by Hampton hotels. Heidi had been in this role for eight years, and according to her direct boss, she was one of the best. She was driven, dissatisfied with mediocrity, guest focused, business savvy, and most important, a passionate advocate for the Hampton brand.

But as you can see from her SET score, she was also burning out.

So there's the rub. Heidi was a talented, intelligent, and ambitious person working for a great company that genuinely wanted the best for its customers and its employees. Yet somehow, despite everybody's best intentions, she'd managed to fall far off her strengths path, a fate that, as you now know, awaits more than eight out of ten of us.

Heidi couldn't put her finger on when it happened, or even quite why it happened, but lately work had started to feel a lot like *work*. Slowly, in incremental doses, Heidi's control of her day had slipped away from her. She would begin her week with a long list of things she wanted to accomplish, and yet, as the week progressed, constant interruptions from annoying people and unexpected tasks would distract her from her list.

She increasingly found herself calling up general managers of struggling hotels and cajoling them to fix a particular problem or sign up for a required corporate program. "Chasing hotels," she called it, and each week it seemed to take up more and more of her time. Most of these struggling general managers wouldn't call her back, and even when they did, they rarely followed through on the requests she made of them. Besides, these conversations weren't pleasant. Heidi loved to challenge people to take her ideas to the next level, but this didn't even come close, having to remind them of basic things they weren't doing and should be, and asking why weren't they, and when would they. She didn't want to have these conversations at all, yet she felt she had to. If she didn't chase these hotels, no one else would, and then, hotel by hotel, the Hampton brand would start to lose its luster. As a devoted Hamptonite, she couldn't stomach this, and so she kept chasing.

She was starting to feel trapped. Hers was a mission she believed in, and always would, but right now her weeks at work were doubly frustrating: Her to-do list wasn't getting done, and instead her time was being taken up with activities that dragged her down. As she looked to the future, she felt one notch less creative, one ounce less resilient than she used to be, at once busier and less effective than at any time in her career.

Her version of a career meltdown wasn't a particularly dramatic affair. She never got to the point where she was throwing TV sets from upper-story hotel rooms or taking up extreme sports like bungee jumping or swimming with sharks to jolt her out of her job woes. Nonetheless, her problems at work were taking an insidious toll on her attitude, and it was weighing on her private life. Her world at work was slowly sinking beneath the weight of activities that were necessary but, to her, frustrating and depleting, and she sensed that without some kind of radical change, she would sink with it.

What was so perplexing about the corruption of her days and weeks at work was that the incremental nature of the process made it extremely difficult to diagnose exactly what was wrong. She knew she was stuck in a rut, but no matter how hard she tried to change her attitude toward her job, she always found herself back at miserable. To make things worse, she started to doubt whether she deserved to be happy at work and couldn't quiet the nagging thoughts that crept into her mind: "Why should I expect to have a job where I do what I love? Sure, my working life is unfulfilling, but is it unbearable? Some people have it far worse, right?"

Heidi was not naive. She didn't believe that work was supposed to elevate her to a state of 100 percent blissed-out happiness. Over the years she tried to find comfort in the notion that tough times at work were just a by-product of the employment contract, and like most of us, she merely hoped she would have more good days than bad ones. Yet when Heidi thought about how she actually spent her time at work, it was clear her scale was tipped severely the wrong way. While she could sometimes rationalize that work is called "work" for a reason, she refused to be passive about her growing disengagement.

Was she managing her time poorly? she wondered. Or after eight years, was she simply done with this role and with this stage of her career? Maybe she should take a break. But then again, perhaps it was the opposite: Maybe she should put in more hours, cram more in, and work her way out of the hole.

She didn't know. And so, even though she didn't like where the needles pointed on her SET dials, she knew she couldn't lie to herself. "Something must change," she told herself, vaguely but with great conviction.

Throughout the book, we'll follow Heidi as she strives to find her way back onto her strengths path. We will see how she succeeds in turning this vague conviction that something must change into a weekly discipline that leads her toward that thing we all covet: a job where we can give our best where we have the best to give; a job where we can flourish.

Heidi's journey began, as yours must, by facing up to something truly strange: namely, that the reason she didn't have a job that capitalized on her strengths was because, on some unspoken level, she didn't really want one.

THE THREE MYTHS

To start your journey, you must at least consider the possibility that what's stopping you from becoming one of the two out of ten is not that your manager won't listen to you, or that the company has pigeonholed you, or that your current job won't let you—although each of those external circumstances may play some role.

You must consider the possibility that what's stopping you is what you believe; that in effect *you* are stopping yourself. Over the years you have come to believe some things, and these beliefs are now so deeply entrenched that no matter what new discipline you learn, and no matter how favorable your circumstances become, you will never make the most of your strengths. Your problem is not that you don't know how to or that no one will let you. It's that you aren't even trying.

Back in 2001, *Now, Discover Your Strengths* quoted a poll showing that when people were prompted with the idea of building on their strengths, and then asked to choose between building on strengths and fixing weaknesses, only 41 percent of Americans chose building on their strengths as the key to success. This same poll revealed that other countries were even less interested in their strengths than the United States. For example, in the UK and Canada, only 38 percent believed that their strengths would drive their success, whereas in Japan and China, this number dipped all the way down to 24 percent.

In 2006, my company asked the same question as part of an effort to measure just how far the hoped-for strengths revolution had come, and the data came back exactly the same. When asked "Which will help you be most successful: building on your strengths or fixing your weaknesses?" 41 percent said "building strengths," and 59 percent said "fixing weaknesses." The needle hadn't moved even one decimal place. In fact, the entire data set was so similar to the original poll that our first thought was that we had accidentally switched the files and were looking at six-year-old results!

No such luck. The files were up-to-date. There was no getting around the data. When we presented people with a choice between building on strengths or fixing weaknesses—and, yes, of course, both are important, but if you were to come down on one side or the other, even if it was just marginally on one side, which would it be?—we found that most respondents would bet their success, their career, and their contribution on fixing weaknesses.

Why? Why are so many of us still drawn to learning those things we lack?

I'm sure you have your own theory: the school system taught us to; we are drawn to our weaknesses because they are the weakest links in our chain, and when they fail, we fail; it's just easier to fix a weakness than to build on a strength.

Mine is that over the years a majority of us have come to believe in certain myths—three, to be precise—three myths that our parents told us were true, that our teachers reinforced, and that today we hear in one form or another from our managers. These myths have become so ingrained in our lives that we no longer see them. They are core assumptions that even now we are passing on to our children, our students, and our employees, and we are pleased with ourselves for doing so.

I don't know if you've read the previous books I've written, so I don't know if you consider yourself to be one of the 41 percent who put their faith in strengths, or one of the 59 percent diligently shoring up their weaknesses. Whichever you are, look at these myths square on before you continue reading. Even though you may have encountered these myths before and wrestled them to the ground, don't declare victory quite yet. Examine them closely. Investigate why they are so attractive to so many of us. Try to be as objective as possible in assessing just how influential they still are in your life and in the lives of those around you. According to the data, in a room of ten people, at least six believe them to be true. If you aren't one of the six, it's going to fall to you to persuade the others to see the not-so-common sense of capitalizing on strengths.

To help you bust each myth and figure out the best way to get a friend or colleague to bust them too, here are three questions that should prove revealing. I encourage you to write down your answers after reading each myth. Later, when you're trying to persuade others, use these questions as a way to begin your discussion:

1. **How does the myth serve you?** There's a reason why each myth insinuates itself so completely into our lives. Only by understanding how the myth helps people get through their day can you start to see how they can be disentangled from it.
2. **What would it cost you to stop believing in this myth?** Since the myths serve us, to stop believing in them will require

that we give up some things. These things are presumably quite precious; otherwise each myth would prove much easier to dislodge. Before we can think about what we will gain by changing our beliefs, we first have to fess up to what we will lose.

3. **How would it benefit you to believe the truth?** This one's the kicker. Our answer had better be compelling enough to allow us to see past our answer to the previous question, otherwise our chances of living a strong life fall to next to nothing. After all, why bother fighting to live a strong life if we can't even describe the benefits? But on the flip side, if we can capture in detail what we will gain by carving a life around our strengths, we'll keep fighting for it for the rest of our lives.

With all that said, consider the first myth:

Myth	As you grow, your personality changes.

Sixty-six percent of us believe this to be true. And on the surface it seems so commonsensical that it's hard to believe it's not true. "Of course I changed as I grew up. I learned new skills. I learned from my experiences. I acquired a broader perspective on myself and the world around me. I became more self-aware, more self-assured, more balanced, wiser, more mature. I put away my childish things and became an adult."

This myth is so interwoven into our culture that we have literally mythologized it in all those retellings of Charles Dickens's story about poor old Scrooge, *A Christmas Carol.* We love those stories of transformation, where the hero starts off grumpy and unpopular, yet by the end he's transformed himself into the friendliest, most generous guy on the block; or his initial overconfidence eventually blossoms into self-awareness. And our love stems from insecurity. When we look in the mirror in the morning, we all are aware—some of us more dimly than others—of an aspect of our personality that we don't like; some part of us we would like to change. And we favor these stories because they reassure us that if we just buckled down and worked at it, we could transform ourselves and become the person we always wanted to be.

These stories help us dream. They inspire us and comfort us, and that's why they can make such great literature, great theater, and, occasionally, great movies.

But they aren't true. They're just stories.

The truth is that as you grow, you don't change into someone else. You don't change your personality. The truth is this:

TRUTH	**AS YOU GROW, YOU BECOME MORE OF WHO YOU ALREADY ARE.**

Have you ever heard of the fundamental attribution error? It sounds comic-book scary, like something Scotty would warn Captain Kirk about on TV's *Star Trek,* but it refers simply to our tendency to attribute a person's behavior to her consistent underlying personality rather than to the demands of her situation. The classic experiment that reveals this error is one where the subjects have a short face-to-face conversation with a person who they think is a researcher but is actually a plant. She has been instructed to act in a very friendly manner to half the subjects and unfriendly to the other half. A little while later, the subjects fill out a questionnaire in which, among other things, they are asked describe the "researcher'"s personality. Naturally the ones she acted friendly toward judge that she has a very pleasant personality, while the others believe her personality to be hostile and critical.

The surprise comes when the experiment is repeated. This time the subjects are told in advance that the researcher has been asked to behave in a friendly way to some of them and in an unfriendly way to others. Despite this very explicit heads-up about why she behaves the way she does, the results remain the same. Those to whom she has been friendly say her personality is friendly, while those to whom she's been standoffish say that she is by nature standoffish.

This experiment has been tried in a variety of different forms and settings, and it always produces the same results. Even when the subjects are told that the researcher's behavior has been dictated by her role in the experiment, they still wind up attributing her behavior to her underlying personality, which is clearly—in the case of this experiment, anyway—a fundamental attribution error.

It is an error in the context of this experiment. But it is not an error in real life. In real life, it's good judgment. In real life, it is wise not only to look to a person's behavior for clues to his underlying personality, but also, once we spot these clues, it is wise to conclude that his underlying personality will be consistent across time and situations. It is wise to believe in this thing called personality and to act as though each person's remains stable.

Why? Because as the fundamental attribution error experiment shows, we all do it. In fact so strong is our instinct to do it, that even when we are all but told not to, we still do it. An instinct this universal and this strong must have value. Sure, it may occasionally lead us astray, but for it to be so prevalent and powerful, it must prove to be a good strategy most of the time. Over millennia, our forebears who acted as though people had consistent and stable personalities must have been more likely to survive and pass on their genes than those unfortunates who didn't. In the language of natural selection, it is an adaptive strategy. It works.

Personality tests confirm this. Much as we might like to believe that we change as we grow, if we take a personality test twice separated by many years, the results from the two tests are almost exactly the same. Not 100 percent the same, to be sure, but where a perfect correlation is 1.0, the results of personality tests taken years apart are in the 0.7 to 0.9 range. For example, when we did this with StrengthsFinder, the test-retest correlations hovered around 0.75—extraordinarily close. (This may occasionally lead to one of a person's top five talents being switched out for a new one, but still, the underlying pattern of responses remains consistent over time.)

The personality tests of identical twins raised apart are even more intriguing. These results reveal that the personality of identical twins, even when raised in different families, cultures, and countries, are startlingly similar—with correlations at the 0.7 level. But they also reveal that if you keep testing the twins over decades, even though they never meet, their personalities become increasingly similar. As they mature, the common grooves of their personality deepen, and they each become more and more of who the other is.

Persuasive though this research is, many of us don't need it. Many of us have kids, and our kids make the point. My son Jackson is five years old, and already I know some things about him. For example, I know that Jack is passionately competitive. Not in the way that most kids are, with their vague preference for winning over losing, but in a deep-and-abiding-hatred-of-losing kind of way. If he's watching his favorite football team on television and they start to lose, he can't stay in the room. He is compelled to run into the other room and bury his face in the sofa cushions. It's a physical thing. His need to win is such an overwhelming force that, once it's triggered, he doesn't know quite what to do with himself.

Last year, as a special reward for being nice to his younger sister for a week, I took him to watch the Arizona State Sun Devils play the Rutgers Scarlet Knights in the Insight Bowl. I picked this football game, first, because ASU was his favorite team. I'm still not entirely sure why. And second, because I judged ASU more of a football powerhouse than Rutgers, so I was pretty sure I could guarantee a win for "our" team.

All went well in the run-up to the game. I had been worried that Jack would be frightened by the extravaganza of a full-blast college bowl game, but he seemed unfazed by it all. The parachutists with smoke pouring out of their heels, the pregame fireworks, the marching bands, the huge inflatable helmets with the teams bursting onto the field through clouds of colored smoke—it was all fun and games for Jackson, perched on my lap with his little Sun Devils cap on.

Until, that is, the game started. ASU stalled on its first possession. Rutgers got the ball and quickly scored a touchdown. ASU turned the ball over again, and Rutgers scored another touchdown. Then ASU turned the ball over *again,* and so there we were, seven minutes in, our team down 14–0, and no offense in sight.

And we had to leave the stadium.

It began with a small, polite "Dad, can we please leave?" Which prompted a calming "Oh, don't worry Jack, ASU will rally" from me. But then things escalated. Not to screaming and shouting and carrying on. He's not that kind of kid. But as the minutes ticked by, and as ASU continued to struggle, Jack became more and more agitated. He twisted in my lap; a distressed, squirming, unhappy little creature burying his head in my shoulder. Then came a barely audible whimper: "Please, please, Dad, can we leave?"

Which, of course, we did. I can take a hint. We left at the end of the first quarter and wound up watching the rest of the game in our hotel room across the street, where the lack of atmosphere was more than made up for by our ability to grab the remote and flip the channel whenever ASU's fortunes took a turn for the worse. (Jackson's happy ending: ASU won 45–40 on a last-minute touchdown.)

I wish I could have persuaded him to walk back into the stadium, particularly after ASU came back to take the lead in the second half, but Jack was having none of it. He feels losing as a physical pain, and he needs—really, truly needs—to be able to shut it off if, God forbid, it starts to happen. That's Jack. And that will always be Jack. My wife and I didn't cause him to be this way, but as far back as I can remember, he was this way, and he always will be.

He won't grow out of this. He won't come to believe that winning and losing are childish concerns. Sure, when he grows up, his competitiveness will manifest itself differently than it does now, but regardless of how much fun the "taking part" is, he will never be able to ignore the outcome. When, as an adult, he learns a new skill, his first thought will still be "What's the score?" as it was last week when he picked up a ping-pong paddle for the first time:

"There's no score, Jack. You have to learn to hit it back before we can start scoring."

"Oh." Pause. "What's the score, Dad?"

Likewise, if some time in the future it happens that he works in an environment where there is no way to measure his performance, no way to compare it to others, he will still feel as frustrated as he now does playing T-ball where, because of tournament rules, every game must end in a tie. ("What was the score, Dad? Fifteen to fifteen? *Again?*")

Today he races his sister every night down the corridor leading to his bedroom. She darts, he chases. Stimulus/response. Twenty years from now, when you walk down a corridor with Jack, he will still be subliminally aware of being just a couple of inches ahead of you. In fact if you were to gradually increase your pace, you might actually be able to get him to break into a run.

Jack's challenge as an adult will not be to put aside this competitiveness and replace it with a more "mature" trait, such as collegiality or team spirit. Instead, his challenge will be to find a productive way to channel this need to win. I hope, as he grows, that he finds ways to focus his competitiveness. I hope he learns to seek out situations in which he can win. And I hope he stops crying when he loses.

But I don't expect he will ever lose his craving to win. I don't expect he will ever learn to be a good loser. Of course, as a parent, I hope that he will learn to be a gracious loser, someone who can be polite in defeat. But Jack is today, and will always be, one of those people who thinks to himself, "You show me a good loser, and I'll show you a *loser.*"

Clearly, I am not suggesting he will experience no change as he grows. His dreams will change. His skills will change. His achievements will change. His circumstances will change, and along with them, I'm sure, his values will change. But the core of him, the most dominant aspects of his personality, will remain the same.

So will yours. And that's OK. That's as it should be. As you grow, your goal should not be to transform yourself, to somehow conjure new forces from within you. Instead your goal should be to free up and focus the forces already there.

So there's the myth, and there's the case for a different kind of truth. I hope the case was persuasive, but regardless, most people—66 percent of people, as you'll recall—don't believe it. If you're going to persuade these people to see things differently, you first need to know why this myth proves so useful.

1. How does it serve you to believe that as you grow your personality changes?

Start by asking this question. Start with yourself, and then, if you're sure you've moved beyond this myth, ask it of those you are striving to persuade. Here are the answers I hear most often:

"It gives me hope that I can keep growing. And, besides, I think I've really changed since I was a kid."

"It allows me to believe in my unlimited potential."

"It allows me to see solutions in the future and to look past a present that I'm not very happy with."

"It lets me not delve too deeply into who I am. Why bother, when I am just going to change anyway?"

"It lets me believe that I'm not trapped by the worst aspects of my personality; that I can rise above them if I just work at it."

When you hear these answers, or when you find yourself thinking them, don't try to counter them immediately. You'll soon get either into some kind of philosophical discussion about whether change is possible or into a detailed debate about some aspect of the person's (or your) personality and whether she has indeed become more gregarious—or more self-assured, or more charming, or a more effective public speaker—than she was when she was a kid. Which, by the way, she probably has. Each of us is an adaptable creature. We can get a little better at virtually anything if it is important enough to us. But getting a little better at something than you were before doesn't necessarily mean that you've changed the distinctive peaks and valleys of your personality. You may have raised the valleys a wee bit, but they're still valleys.

No one likes to hear this, though, so unless you want a fight, don't lead with this argument. Instead, ask the next question:

2. What would it cost you to stop believing that your personality changes as you grow?

This question always yields interesting answers:

"It would cost me my belief that life's a journey."

"It would cost me something I have been certain of my entire life."

"It would cost me my belief that progress is always possible."

"It would cost me my belief that learning and growing are critical to success."

And, for the more theologically inclined:

"It would cost me my belief in original sin, my belief that the journey of life is the journey of rising above the flaws of my personality and the striving for a more generous, more graceful way of being."

Since life is indeed a journey, and progress is possible, and each of us can indeed live more generously and gracefully, there's no countering these answers. Best to allow them to be aired and then simply ask the third question. Naturally the most persuasive answers are the ones a person arrives at himself.

3. How would it benefit you to believe that as you grow, you become more of who you already are?

"I would be able to put my trust in me rather than in something outside of me."

"That no one will ever make quite the same contribution as me."

"I would be able to stop listening to my parents, my teachers, or my boss telling me what I should strive for, and instead I would be able to start listening to a voice I know really well: my own."

"That the answers to the really big questions in my life—What should I do with my life? Where will I excel? Where will I make the greatest impact?—can be found within my own experience . . . if I know where to look."

"That I have far more control in terms of my career and my contribution than I thought."

On the next page you'll find space to write down your own answers. The reason why so many people hang on to this first myth is that it is comforting. So take the time to formulate your answers. Think through your relationship to this myth. Use these three questions to reveal how as it comforts, it limits.

Whatever you hear when you ask these questions, remember: none of it means that you cannot grow. Of course you can,

1. How does it serve you to believe that as you grow your personality changes?

2. What would it cost you to stop believing this?

3. How would it benefit you to believe that as you grow, you become more of who you already are?

and you will. But here we run smack into the second of the three myths:

Myth	You will grow the most in your areas of greatest weakness.

Sixty-one percent of people believe this to be true, and it's possible that you are one of them. If so, your indoctrination in this myth started very early. In kindergarten, if you were proficient in English but struggled with math, you didn't get more English classes, you got remedial math. And your parents were in on the game. As they scanned your report cards, there was the momentary pause to congratulate you on your list of As and Bs before they got down to the serious business of dissecting why you received that one F and what exactly you were planning to do about it. Perhaps your parents weren't quite this remedial. If so, they are the exception. As repeated polls have revealed, when asked what they spend most time talking about with their child, her As, Cs, or Fs, more than 70 percent of parents say the Fs.

The point here isn't that parents should ignore the Fs, anymore than you should ignore your own weaknesses. Sometimes you just have to dig in and try to get a little better—especially if it is the only way to get promoted to the next year's grade. The point is simply that you will not learn and grow the most in your areas of weakness. Instead you will learn and grow the *least* in your areas of weakness, and what learning and growth you do achieve will be hard won. This is as true of you today as it was when you were five.

When I was growing up, I had many weaknesses. One of them was my fear of confrontation. No matter how carefully I rehearsed what I was going to say to my dad, no matter how carefully I planned my arguments, my examples, and my precedents, when it actually came time to have the conversation with him, my brain would somehow shut down my mouth, and the words would stick fast in my throat.

When I joined the world of work, people soon recognized this trait. They would take me under their wing and counsel me, saying, "Marcus, in the business world, you have to drag the elephant out from under the table and deal with it." And they'd quote little aphorisms to motivate me to do better, such as "Confrontation is the first step toward resolution." And they'd send me off to assertiveness-training classes so that I could learn the tried-and-true confrontation tricks, such as "Always look the person in the eye if you want to intimidate him" or "If you want to throw someone off his game, then, as he raises his voice, deliberately lower yours." Frankly, it was all good stuff, and all very well meaning on their part, and I took their advice seriously. I worked at it and worked at it, and truth be told, I did indeed get better. In the area of confrontation, I went from terrible to just bad.

In the grand scheme of things, this was not a particularly good use of my time.

A far better use would have been to invest all this energy, diligence, and focus in my strengths. And of course the same applies to you. This is the truth you should live your life by:

TRUTH	**YOU WILL GROW THE MOST IN YOUR AREAS OF GREATEST STRENGTH.**

You may not be creative in all aspects of your life, but whatever your general level of creativity may be, you will be at the peak of your creative powers in your areas of strength. You may not be a naturally inquisitive person, but you will be at your most inquisitive in your areas of strength. You will be most optimistic, most courageous, and most ambitious when playing to an area of strength. And when you hit resistance or obstacles to your goals, you will bounce back fastest when those goals center on one of your strengths.

If you take nothing else away from this book, take this: You have development needs—areas where you need to grow, areas where you need to get better—but for you, as for all of us, you will learn the most, grow the most, and develop the most in your areas of greatest strength. Your strengths are your multiplier. Your strengths magnify you.

Why is this so? Why isn't it equally true that you will grow the most in your areas of weakness? Why, with all my diligent effort at becoming better at confrontation, wasn't my brain sufficiently malleable for me to go from terrible to fantastic?

One answer is just biology. When you learn and grow and come up with new ideas, the biological underpinnings of this are the creation of new synaptic connections in your brain. As I described in my most recent book, *The One Thing You Need to Know*, it takes significant infrastructure to grow new synapses. Genes have to be switched on, proteins created, blood vessels built. Since nature doesn't want to build infrastructure unnecessarily, she looks for ways to exploit preexisting infrastructure. In other words, she finds it easier to create new synaptic connections in those areas of your brain where you already have abundant synaptic connections. You grow the most where you are already strong.

But this just begs another why? Why did nature make us so that it's far easier to learn and grow in our areas of strength?

The answer can be found in all the twins studies conducted over the last couple of decades by behavioral geneticists. Their results are intriguing and will more than likely fly in the face of what you've been taught about why you have the personality you do, and why your personality is so different from those of your siblings, cousins, and friends.

For example, we can now finally lay to rest the age-old question about which has more influence on who you are: nature or nurture. In every study of its kind, the results are always the same: 45 to 50 percent of your personality is nature. That is to say 45 to 50 percent of your personality is due to the genes that you inherited from your mother and your father. I realize that this sounds impossibly precise, but if you gather enough personality-test results from identical twins raised together, and results from those raised apart; and a similarly large number of results from fraternal twins and nontwin siblings raised together and apart; *and* the personality test results from the parents of all these children—getting all these results is the hard part—then the work of calculating how much of each child's personality is inherited is, mathematically speaking, quite straightforward.

And what of the remaining 50 to 55 percent? Well, we used to think that this remainder was due to nurture—how you were weaned, potty trained, disciplined, praised, whether you were in day care or not, where you were in the birth order of your siblings, and so on.

We now know this isn't true. How you were raised has absolutely no impact on your personality at all. Just to be clear, *0* percent of the remaining 50 to 55 percent is determined by how your parents raised you. (Judith Rich Harris's book *No Two Alike* provides an incisive description of these studies and their challenging implications.)

This doesn't mean that your parents' behavior and your relationship with them are unimportant. On the contrary, not only do they surround us with the unconditional love for which we all yearn (that is, if they are effective parents), they also affect many specific aspects of you and your behavior, such as your religious beliefs, your manners, your support of the Arizona State Sun Devils, your fascination with Chris Martin of the band Coldplay, your love of soccer, and your appetite for Granny's special shepherd's pie dinner.

But as long as their behavior falls within the bounds of normal parenting (if there was abuse or repeated trauma in your childhood, these obviously leave their scars), how your parents weaned you or disciplined you or praised you does not affect your personality at all. And by *personality*, I mean it will not affect how competitive you are, or how timid, or how patient, or how outgoing, or how self-assured, or how willful, or how creative, or how focused, or how responsible, or how calm, or how positive, or any other trait that might apply to you.

Again, to be clear, this doesn't imply that parents don't matter. It simply means that which family you were brought up in has no measurable impact on your personality.

And neither, contrary to recent books on the subject, does birth order. Parents think it does because they are very familiar with their children's behavior inside the home and consequently witness many examples of how elder siblings react to the younger ones, and how each child is subtly different from the others. Because parents are also acutely aware of the birth order of their children, they then draw conclusions that link a child's behavior to his birth order.

I know I did this. Jackson, I always said, was a typical first child. He was slower to warm up to people, quite highly strung, sensitive, and, to his younger sister, alternately dominating and parental. My daughter Lilia, with her winning, joyful, oh-what-a-happy-day ways, was a typical second child.

Studies now reveal not that my character assessments are wrong—Jackson and Lilia do indeed behave in the ways I've just described—but that they behave *most* like this in only two situations: namely, in the home and around each other. Separate them or get them in school, and the distinct patterns of behavior that I know so well, and that I've long ascribed to birth order, become much less defined. So much so that in studies where children's behavior is monitored and their personality measured outside of the home—by teachers, for example—there is no correlation whatsoever between personality and birth order.

So if it's not parenting, and it's not birth order, what *does* affect the remaining 50 to 55 percent of your personality? An overwhelming body of research suggests that two forces are at play (again, I'll refer you to Judith Rich Harris's book if you want to dive into the data itself):

a. Chance, which can mean pretty much anything, from your bad luck in suffering repeated ear infections as a child, to the random variations in your genes as you grow. (These small variations explain why we sometimes see one identical twin with a cleft palate, while the other, although genetically identical, does not have one, or why it's possible for one twin to be a schizophrenic, and not the other.)
b. Your peers.

Not peers in the clichéd sense of peer pressure. You may well have felt some peer pressure growing up, but if you did, this will have affected only your behavior and your values, and probably only temporarily. Peer pressure of this kind will not affect your underlying personality.

I mean peers in the sense that your peers are the most reliable sources of information about you and, in particular, about what your true strengths are in the world outside your home. Your peers will tell you accurately (far more accurately than your family will) if and who you can dominate, if you're funny, if and when you're a good ally, if your ideas are interesting, if your ideas are practical, if you are trustworthy, and so on.

This is tremendously valuable information for you as a child, since it helps you learn where you have the best chance to compete successfully as an adult. So from birth through early adolescence, you are wired, as are all humans in all cultures, to seek out feedback from your peer group as to where your relative strengths lie.

While you are picking up on these clues about your strengths, a second system kicks in. This system pushes you to seek out situations where you can play to these strengths, and these repeated behaviors cause material changes in your brain development, which in turn cause you to play to your strengths still more. This system continues to do its work throughout your childhood and early adolescence. Then, once you reach your mid teens, it locks these changes in.

These, then, were the instructions written into your biological design specs when you were born, which we can state as follows:

1. Pay very close attention to what your childhood peers think of you.
2. Identify where you have some preexisting strengths in relation to these peers.
3. Build on these strengths, and then
4. *Permanently* skew your personality toward these strengths while you are still a young teenager.

Nature makes sure you are born different, and then, not content with this, it has designed a complex feedback and personality-molding system to ensure that you become even more different. It wants you both to seek out your strengths and then to strengthen these strengths.

Why did nature design you this way? The same reason it gave you an adaptive immune system and opposable thumbs. Because you're more competitive this way. Find your natural advantages, then seek out unoccupied niches where you can capitalize on these advantages, and you are more likely to thrive, whether in a group of hunter-gatherers or a team of coworkers. Specialization: It's nature's strategy for winning.

All right, these are all sound arguments for why you will grow the most in your areas of greatest strength. But rationality doesn't always, nor even often, carry the day. The myth that you'll grow the most in your areas of weakness persists in informing the way we raise our children, the way we teach our students, and the way we train our employees, because, on an emotional level, it just seems right. So to uproot it, you must confront the emotional anchors holding it in place.

To help you, stop reading for a moment and return to those three myth-busting questions. We don't want to influence your answers, but to get your wheels turning, here are the answers we hear most frequently:

1. How does it serve you to believe that you will grow the most in your areas of greatest weakness?

"My weaknesses can hurt me and those around me—my customers, my colleagues, my boss, my friends, even my family. If I learn to improve my weaknesses, I will feel more well rounded and less vulnerable."

"Working on those things I struggle with makes me feel responsible."

"It's easier to see improvement when the starting point is so low."

"Fixing something I'm bad at seems like a necessity, so it gives me the motivation to get off the dime and take action."

"It reinforces what I've always been taught."

"By believing this, I fit in. It encourages me to do what everybody tells me I should do."

2. What would it cost you to stop believing this?

"I want people to see me as a good soldier. If I stop fixing my weaknesses, it could cost me their approval."

"I've always prided myself on my work ethic. I'm the kind of person who's never satisfied, who always wants to get better. I would have to give this up."

"I manage people. The 'fix-weaknesses' mind-set was time efficient. I just looked to where each person was struggling and then put together a plan for how he could improve. The 'build-strength' mind-set seems far more time consuming."

3. How would it benefit you to believe that you will grow the most in your areas of greatest strength?

"I will get to challenge myself in those areas of my work that I already love to do."

"I will be able to indulge my natural curiosity."

"I will see myself get better faster—exponential improvement rather than incremental."

"I will get to excel and be seen as an expert in one or two key areas."

"I will be on the cutting edge of new developments and trends in a few areas of my job."

"I will come to be viewed as a person who comes up with new ideas and innovations."

Although we hear these answers often, they may not be yours. So, over to you:

1. How does it serve you to believe that you will grow the most in your areas of greatest weakness?

2. What would it cost you to stop believing this?

3. How would it benefit you to believe that you will grow the most in your areas of greatest strength?

Whatever answers these questions yield, you may wind up thinking: "I would love to play to my strengths. I would love to spend most of my time refining and sharpening my strengths, but I can't. I don't have the luxury. I work on a team, and the team needs more from me. The team needs me to put aside my strengths and do whatever it takes to help the team win. Surely this is the right, most responsible thing for me to do as a team member."

Well, no. This perspective, though honorable and well intended, is flawed. It's actually the third and final myth that might be holding you back from becoming one of the two out of ten. Whereas the previous myth was a rational myth, causing you to misjudge that you will net the greatest return from investing in your weaknesses, this one is a moral myth and therefore can be even more entrenched. It says:

Myth	A good team member does whatever it takes to help the team.

Ninety-one percent of people believe this to be true, and it's easy to see why. Again, you were indoctrinated in this one very early. On every school team, coaches preached the message that "this isn't about you, it's about the team," that you can't win by yourself, that you need to be unselfish, that "there's no *I* in team."

And the indoctrination continues in the larger business world, where you are regularly subjected to team-building exercises and company retreats presided over by facilitators cut from the same cloth as your coaches. You're told to be flexible, adaptable, well rounded, always ready and willing to step in and play whatever role the team may need you to play.

The reality is a little different. The truth is that while you will certainly accomplish more if you collaborate with your teammates—there's no question that teams are more effective than groups of disconnected individuals—when you look closely at the most effective teams, you discover that the players on these teams are not well rounded. They are not chipping in and doing whatever the team requires of them. Instead they are living by this truth:

> **TRUTH** **A GOOD TEAM MEMBER DELIBERATELY VOLUNTEERS HIS STRENGTHS TO THE TEAM MOST OF THE TIME.**

They have realized that the right, most responsible thing to do is to identify where their strengths lie, and then to figure out how to arrange their time and their role so that they play to these strengths most of the time. They have then taken it upon themselves to seek out others on the team who are strong where they are weak. Thus the team is well rounded, precisely because each of the players is not.

Sure, occasionally each team member will have to step outside of his strengths zone and "pinch-hit" for the team. But as every effective coach soon realizes, this isn't the essence of teamwork, it's the exception to it. True teamwork occurs only when a complementary set of strengths comes together in a coordinated whole.

This can be frighteningly hard to achieve, not least because it requires a coach/manager who has an eye for each person's unique configuration of strengths and weaknesses. But it is virtually impossible to achieve if you don't take your own strengths seriously. The team doesn't need from you some vague willingness to "do whatever it takes." It needs you to understand your strengths and weaknesses in vivid detail and then take it upon yourself to figure out how to navigate toward the strengths and away from the weaknesses.

What this actually sounds like is you saying to your colleagues, "I need to do more of these specific activities because they play to my strengths, and less of these, because they don't." You may balk at saying this because, frankly, it sounds self-centered and inconsiderate, even irresponsible. But try to talk yourself through these initial feelings.

It isn't irresponsible. Your teammates need to know where they can rely on you the most. The most responsible thing you can do is tell them, and your strengths are the answer.

It isn't inconsiderate. Just because you don't like doing certain activities doesn't mean that all people dislike them the way you do. I loathe confrontation and would be permanently depleted by a working day filled with it. But other people seem to get a kick out of it. It's not inconsiderate of me to hand off confrontation to someone like this; it's practical.

And it isn't self-centered. To assume that everyone loves and loathes the same things you do, and that your team should parcel out the responsibilities according to your pattern of loves and loathes—*this* is self-centered. To assume that each person is wired a little differently, that what makes you feel weak might actually make someone else feel strong, and that your team should capitalize on these differences—this is, well, true.

It may be true, but fewer than 10 percent of us fully embrace it. So, one last time, ask yourself those three myth-busting questions. Here they are, accompanied, as a catalyst for you, by the most common responses:

1. How does it serve you to believe that a good team member does whatever it takes to help the team?

"It makes me feel more secure on the team. After all, if I needed help from one of my colleagues, I would want him to chip in and do whatever it takes to help me, even if it wasn't in his area of strength."

"It reinforces my view of the world. My parents, teachers, and coaches have always told me this was true."

"It makes me popular with my teammates. They like it that I have got their back."

2. What would it cost you to stop believing this?

"It would cost me the approval of my teammates."

"It would cost me the good feelings I get when I sacrifice and do something I don't like to do for the good of the team. Life isn't always a bed of roses."

"It would cost me performance. Sometimes the team just needs me to knuckle down and get something done. When these times come, I can't ignore them."

3. How would it benefit you to believe that a good team member volunteers his strengths to the team most of the time?

"Deep down, it's what I want to do for the team most of the time anyway."

"I will come to be respected as a person who delivers in crunch time."

"The more success I have in playing to my strengths on the team, the more the team will rework its 'playbook' to call upon my strengths."

1. How does it serve you to believe that you should chip in and do whatever it takes to help the team?

2. What would it cost you to stop believing this?

3. How would it benefit you to believe that you should deliberately volunteer your strengths to the team most of the time?

"I will be able to stop having to volunteer for projects that I know don't play to my strengths."

Obviously, I don't know what your answers to these myth-busting questions were, but please take the time to write them down. Your journey toward living a strong life will be challenging enough. It will be nigh on impossible if you haven't first convinced yourself that it's a journey worth making.

And the same applies to the people you work with. "Play to your strengths" is one of those aphorisms that sounds so commonsensical that, when you say it, everyone happily nods his assent. And yet, as we've seen from the data, most of us don't really believe that we can live our life this way. To make this "sense" more commonly held, you're going to have to do your part in persuading those around you to see the wisdom of it. These three questions, and the discussions they create, will prove useful.

For a video challenge from me about Step 1, visit Simply Strengths.com.

Myth	As you grow, your personality changes.

TRUTH	**AS YOU GROW, YOU BECOME MORE OF WHO YOU ALREADY ARE.**

Your values, your skills, your self-awareness, and some of your behaviors may change. But the most dominant aspects of your personality will remain the same.

Myth	You will grow the most in your areas of greatest weakness.

TRUTH	**YOU WILL GROW THE MOST IN YOUR AREAS OF GREATEST STRENGTH.**

You will be the most inquisitive, most resilient, most creative, and most open to learning in your areas of strength.

Myth	A good team member does whatever it takes to help the team.

TRUTH	**A GOOD TEAM MEMBER DELIBERATELY VOLUNTEERS HIS STRENGTHS TO THE TEAM MOST OF THE TIME.**

A great team member is not well rounded. The great team is well rounded, precisely because each great team member is not.

STEP 2

GET CLEAR

"DO YOU KNOW WHAT YOUR STRENGTHS ARE?"

Have you ever noticed that when you ask people to describe their weaknesses, they somehow manage to spin the description around so that the weaknesses sound suspiciously like strengths?

"My weakness is that I care too much."

"I'm too much of a perfectionist."

"My standards are just too high for my own good."

In fact, as I write this, I'm having a hard time remembering a single instance during an interview in which a person just came right out and said, "You know what? I am weak at thinking strategically," or "I struggle with implementing my plans once I've designed them." It must have happened, I suppose, but too rarely to recall.

We shouldn't be too surprised by this, though, because it's human nature to want to put as positive a spin as possible on who we are, at least in terms of how we present ourselves to the outside world. I'm sure I am guilty of it, and perhaps you are too. But given our penchant for positive self-presentation, it is at least understandable.

What is much less easy to understand is why we are so inarticulate when it comes to describing our strengths. Our strengths are the very qualities that could make us look our best, and yet when asked to detail them we lack, well, detail. Our answers tend to verge on the too-generic-to-be-worth-listening-to category. In previous books, I've written that when you ask people to describe their strengths, the most common answer is "I like dealing with people," and the evidence from the intervening years is that this is still true. If we were to bet on what answer we would hear when we ask someone to describe his strengths, this is the answer we'd win money on. There's rarely any mention of *which* people he's good at dealing with—strangers or friends or customers or prospects—and little vividness about what he's actually doing with these people. Is he selling to them, or taking care of them, or coaching them, or calming them down, or inspiring them, or what?

The other one we'd get short odds on is "I'm good at making things happen." But, again, there's hardly ever an accompanying description of exactly what kind of things he's good at making happen; whether he's good at creating the things before he makes them happen versus making things happen only after someone else has made the things; or whether his particular genius is making many little things happen all at once as opposed to following one big thing all the way through to completion. Just "making things happen." That's all we'd likely get.

Many people come to talk to me about their strengths, and exceptions to this blandness often come from people who have taken the Clifton StrengthsFinder profile. When these people describe their strengths, they tend to list five talent themes. (The profile measures you on thirty-four themes of talent, and when you're done, it presents you with your top five.) Since the express purpose of the profile is to provide you with a language to describe the best of yourself, both to you and to others, it's wonderful—from my perspective, at least—to hear you refer back to this language when trying to describe your strengths.

However—and it's a big however—these labels are not your strengths. Your strengths are defined by your actual activities. They are things you do, and more specifically, things you do consistently and near perfectly. Thus, if you are a nurse, one of your strengths might be giving injections that seem almost painless to the patient. Or if you are a front desk clerk in a hotel, one of your strengths might be taking charge of each guest's experience and making him feel like he's in good hands. Or if you are in sales, you might have a strength in closing deals when competing head-to-head.

As noted in *Now, Discover Your Strengths*, strengths such as these are made up of three separate ingredients:

1. Talents, such as empathy, assertiveness, or competitiveness. Since you tend to be so close to your own talents that you take them for granted, the purpose of the Clifton Strengths-Finder and other personality profiles is to help you step back from yourself and put a label on your talents. These talents are things you're born with and they stay with you. That's why your personality-profile results don't change much during your life.
2. Skills, such as knowing the steps involved in giving an injection safely, or how to check a guest into your hotel, or how to do a comparative analysis of your product's features and your competitors' products. Skills are not innate. They can be learned.
3. Knowledge, such as which dosage is correct for a particular patient, or which local restaurant will appeal to a certain guest, or who is your most dangerous competitor in the marketplace. Obviously, knowledge is learned.

As an example, putting these three ingredients together— the talent of empathy, the skill of giving an injection safely, and the knowledge of the right dosage for the patient—creates the strength of "giving injections that seem painless to the patient."

The talent of assertiveness, the skill of checking in a guest, and the knowledge of local restaurants combine to create the strength of "taking charge of each guest's experience."

The talent of competitiveness, the skill of doing a comparative analysis, and the knowledge of your product's competitors combine to create the strength of "closing deals when competing head-to-head."

Defining these ingredients is useful for two reasons. First, it shows you which aspects of your strengths are learnable and which aren't. Second, it reveals which aspects of your strengths you can take with you from situation to situation (namely, your talents), and which aspects tend to be situation specific (namely, your skills and knowledge). Thus, the comparative analysis you did as a salesperson in one industry is unlikely to prove useful if you switch to selling in a different industry, whereas your innate competitiveness will fire you up no matter what you are selling.

However, when it comes time to identify your own strengths, these distinctions between talents, skills, and knowledge are less helpful. To capture the *specific activities* that constitute your strengths, you are going to have to go beyond generic talent labels and pinpoint how your actual activities in a regular week make you feel. Your personality-profile results can certainly prod you into looking in the right direction, but that's all they do. You must then take the next step and pay close attention to your feelings before, during, and after your weekly activities. Only then will you get clear on exactly what your true strengths are.

To help you, here are the four telltale signs of a strength.

THE FOUR SIGNS OF A STRENGTH

The acronym *SIGN* is a good way to organize and remember them. To preview, *S* is for Success, *I* is for Instinct, *G* is for Growth, and *N* is for Needs.

S is for Success

If I were to ask you to describe your strengths, you would more than likely begin with those things at which you feel successful, and, frankly, this is a sensible place to start. For an activity to be labeled a strength, you must obviously have some ability in it, and your success, measured or otherwise, is the best indicator of ability. To be sure, you may not be the most accurate judge of what you're good at—you will probably assess yourself too harshly or too generously depending on how fragile your ego is. Nonetheless, how effective you feel at an activity—your *self-efficacy,* in psychological parlance—is a solid first indicator of a strength.

Don't fix on these activities as strengths quite yet, though. The conventional definition of a strength as "an activity you're good at" is not wrong, it's just incomplete. What it leaves out is all the stuff you really want to know about. You don't really want to know what you're good at. You know this already. It's an outcome, it's already happened, it's in the past. And you don't want to know about the past. You want to know about your future. You want to know where you will improve the most as you train and practice. You want to know where you will be at your most creative and generate the best new ideas. You want to know which activities will fulfill and sustain you as you march on through life. These are the most interesting questions, the answers to which will help you know where you will sustain the greatest performance over time.

There will undoubtedly be some activities at which you are proficient but which don't energize you in the slightest. Fate blessed you with ability but forgot to charge this ability with positive emotions. So you do it, and you do it well, and because you do it well, people keep asking you to do it. In fact they rely on you to do it. But from your perspective, if you never had to do it again, your life would be none the worse.

In fact it might be a whole lot better. I once interviewed a marketing executive, Maggie Lindbergh, who had a knack for organizing complex projects. She would swoop in, gather up all the bits and pieces, sort them out into the right chunks, and then sequence it so that the project flowed smoothly. She was a brilliant arranger. But, perversely, the act of doing so drained her of energy. A day or two of organizing and arranging, and she felt like the smallest thing—a missed deadline, a curt remark—and she would burst into tears. So is bringing order to complex projects a strength of hers? Is it an activity she should steer her time at work toward? Hardly.

Matt Borden presents an even more extreme example. Fate blessed him with an obvious physical ability and then, bizarrely, made him hate it.

When Matt was around six years old, a lifeguard who had been watching him swim at the beach approached his mother and told her that he had a near-perfect freestyle stroke. He thought Matt was such an outstanding natural swimmer that he strongly encouraged her to put him on a swim team. Always looking for a way to release some of his boy energy, Matt's mom found a team and arranged for a tryout.

Matt had a gut reaction to seeing the pool and all the other swimmers filed in lanes, thrashing through what seemed like endless laps. When the coach asked him to do a little freestyle in order to evaluate his form, Matt jumped in the pool and proceeded to pretend he couldn't swim.

More than a little ticked off, Matt's mother marched over to the side of the pool and had words with him. She told him to quit fooling around and to swim the way he normally swam. Feeling his back against the pool wall, Matt complied and transformed his style from the faked near-drowning crawl to the precision human fish flow that was innate to him. The coach invited Matt onto the team.

Soon thereafter, Matt began to amass a collection of medals won in events ranging from sprints to long distances to relays. Freestyle was his best stroke, but Matt was such a natural swimmer that he was a multiple threat in backstroke, butterfly, and breaststroke as well. Of course, despite Matt's natural talent, he still had to train hard, and it was routine for him to log two-hour workouts and thousands of yards every day in both the morning and afternoon.

The problem was that over the years Matt grew to loathe swimming. Even while he was in high school, where as a freshman he made the varsity squad and was the star of the team, his disdain for swimming became so intense that he would get debilitating migraines before meets. It reached a point where he felt that the last time he could remember feeling any joy in the water was that afternoon the lifeguard had spotted him. What made it all the more confusing was that Matt continued to win events and set school records and receive praise from his friends, family, and coaches. He couldn't understand how something he was so good at made him feel so bad. He also didn't know how he could quit something in which he had so much blatant talent.

But there was something else that Matt was good at, and it was something that made him feel . . . well, it made him feel like a rock star. Matt loved playing guitar and writing music. Even when practicing scales over and over, time would flow, and he couldn't wait to drop his newfound licks and skills into his admittedly amateur compositions. Yet he didn't care if his songs were simple, he knew that the formula for a great song was often nothing more than "three chords and the truth," and this was something he was happy to pursue.

He also understood that even when he struggled through a song, it made him feel a way that swimming never did. When Matt played music, he felt more like himself.

So at the end of his junior year in high school, Matt went to his swim coach and told him he was quitting. To his credit, he didn't compromise and wasn't assuaged by the deals his coach and parents tried to make to encourage him to both swim and play music. Matt made his decision and stuck with it.

And sure enough, Matt's paralyzing migraines stopped. Today Matt is a music producer who owns a studio in Southern California. He still plays guitar and also the bass, piano, and drums, and he is particularly good at making first-time singers comfortable in the studio environment so they can deliver inspired vocal tracks. Matt laughs now when he recalls that tryout in which he pretended he couldn't swim. It's part melancholy laughter that seems to acknowledge the childhood wisdom of seeing a future he was trying to avoid, and part relieved laughter that he eventually came to see through the false signs that fate was sending.

Matt's might be an extreme example, but you will have some activities like this: all-ability, no-appetite kinds of activities. You can do them because, like Matt, you've got a natural gift for them, or because you're smart, or you're diligent, or responsible, or all of the above, but you don't want to do them. They bore you, drain you, frustrate you, or worse yet, give you migraines.

Are these your strengths? Should we tell you to invest time and energy learning how to do them even better? Should we tell you to steer your week toward them, to seek out opportunities where they will be needed, to find roles where success depends on them? Of course not.

No, your strengths are more than merely what you're good at. Look closely and you'll spot the other signs of your strengths.

I is for Instinct

Your strengths have an I-can't-help-but quality to them. You can't quite articulate why, but you find yourself drawn to certain activities repeatedly. Even though you may be just a little scared to do them, just a little nervous—"Maybe I'm not good enough, maybe I'll fail"—you nonetheless feel a pull toward them.

As a child, I had some difficulty speaking—a mysterious stammer came upon me when I was five and lasted till beyond my twelfth birthday. Nonetheless, whenever my teachers required a kid to read aloud in class, I would find my hand shooting up as though I were reaching for something. And even though I was frightened of what would happen, that my mouth would fail to perform and I would look stupid—which is what usually did happen—I couldn't stop myself from volunteering. The teacher would ask for a line of a poem to be read and up would go my hand. A casting call for the class play would be announced and there I'd be, first in line.

Inexplicable, really, but you'll be able to identify specific activities such as this. There's no rational accounting for it, but you find yourself instinctively looking forward to doing them. You may feel a twinge of fear, but, unprompted, you put yourself in situations where you will have to perform them.

G is for Growth

By now you know that the biological underpinnings of your strengths are the presence of thick branches of synaptic connections. You also know that because of nature's habit of piggy-backing on existing infrastructure, you will grow the most new synaptic connections in those areas where you already have the most existing ones. Here you will learn the most, come up with the most new ideas, and have the best insights.

So much for biology. The problem is, you can't actually peer inside your brain to identify these thick branches. So what should you be on the lookout for? What does a thicket of synapses firing actually feel like?

It feels easy. It feels like you're not trying very hard. It feels like an activity that, for some reason, proved quite simple for you to pick up. You learned it quickly and now, when you are doing it, you don't struggle to concentrate. Instead you naturally stay focused and time speeds up, and you still stay focused and time speeds up some more. You have to remind yourself to stop and look up at the clock, and when you do, whole hours have flown by.

It feels like interest, and more, it feels like inquisitiveness. It's the activity that you want to practice, to read up on, to refine with new tricks and techniques, to grow.

It feels like true happiness. This sounds odd, but bear with me. I'm not suggesting you are smiling beatifically while you're doing it. You may be, but it's doubtful. A recent spate of academic research into happiness has revealed that most of us are quite unreliable when it comes to predicting what will make us happy. In fact, over the course of our lives, our "happiness-o-meter" appears to move very little. We each have our level, and no matter what happens to us, whether winning the lottery or losing the use of our limbs, after a brief blip either up or down, we seem to return to our preset level of happiness.

But research by Mihaly Csikszentmihalyi, author of the seminal book *Flow*, has shown that happiness and concentration are very closely linked. He and his team of researchers handed out pagers to their subjects, paged them at random intervals throughout the day, and asked them to rate their level of happiness whenever the pager went off. The results from more than ten thousand people, gathered over the last twenty-five years, show that, although our absolute level of happiness won't vary much, each of us is at our personal peak of happiness when we are deeply immersed in a specific activity. Get us involved in a task for which we have a powerful inquisitiveness, and although we may not have predicted we'd be happy doing this activity, when you set off our pager and jolt us out of our deep concentration, our happiness ratings soar.

Happiness and focus. You rarely have one without the other.

"Paradoxically," writes Csikszentmihalyi, "the feeling of happiness is only realized after the event. To acknowledge it at the time would only serve as a distraction—the rock climber would lose his footing, the chess player his game. Out of all the moments pinpointed by people I have interviewed, their best are with hindsight."

It's not that these are activities without effort. There is almost certainly effort, but it is, seemingly, effortless. You feel challenged, but in just the way you like to be challenged. You actually want to concentrate. When you do, you lose your regular perspective— your third eye looking down at yourself assessing how long things are taking and what you are doing and what other people are thinking and when it will be over—and you become immersed. You are lost in the activity, for a long moment.

N is for Needs

The final sign of a strength, the N of SIGN, stands for needs. Whereas the Instinct sign refers to how you feel before you do the activity, and the Growth sign to your feelings during the activity, the Needs sign points to how you feel right after you've done it.

Some activities just seem to fill an innate need of yours. When you're done with them, you may feel physically tired, to the point where you are not yet ready to saddle up and tackle them all over again. But you don't feel psychologically drained. Instead you feel fulfilled, powerful, restored, the exact opposite of drained. It's a satisfying feeling, sure, but it's also much more than mere satisfaction. It feels authentic, correct.

This all-is-right-with-the-world feeling is addictive. Your need to feel it again and again is, to return to the *I* of SIGN, what creates in you the instinct to look forward to the activity, to volunteer for the activity, and to seek out situations where you can do it. You want this feeling again, and you'll put yourself through a lot to get it.

I've done a fair amount of live television in my day, and the consensus is that I'm not too shabby at it. So long as I'm prepared and know exactly what I am going to say, I can acquit myself acceptably well, even on those morning shows like *Good Morning America* and the *Today* show, where they ask you to nail your subject amusingly yet pithily in three minutes while a voice in your earpiece counts down the seconds until the end of the segment.

Yes, I can do it, but when I'm done, I never want to do it again. I feel empty and weak. Bump into me in the greenroom afterward, and my knees have buckled under me and I'm hunched on a couch, the light gone from my eyes, my mind as dull as a lump of lead. I would take any number of red-eye flights across the country to get away from having to do it again.

By contrast, my wife, Jane, would take any flight, at any time of day, no matter how long, for the opportunity to do live television—and this is a woman who hates flying with a passion, whose wild-eyed stares at the slightest turbulence scare the other passengers. She does fifteen or so segments a year for *GMA* as the show's trend correspondent, and even though these segments are unpaid, inconveniently located in New York (we live in Los Angeles), and always involve significant prework, she would happily do fifteen more.

I ask her why, and she struggles to find the right words. It's certainly not the thrill of seeing herself on TV—ironically, she doesn't even watch her own segments. And it's not a generic love of performing—she has her own taped show, *The Modern Girl's Guide to Life,* and filming the show doesn't fulfill her in quite the same pure and intense way that a live segment does. It's something else, something specific to live television. When I push her, she says things like "I feel at my best when that little red light goes on" or "I feel my most *me* when I'm done." Whatever it is, all she knows is that she hears a voice calling her toward something quite specific, and that when she answers, "it just feels right."

YOUR STRENGTHS ARE THOSE ACTIVITIES THAT MAKE YOU FEEL STRONG

Putting these four signs together, the simplest and most useful definition of a strength is this: Your strengths are those activities that make you feel strong. (The flip side is also true: "An activity that makes you feel weak" is the best definition of a weakness. More on this in step four.) This definition captures the insight that how you feel while you are doing an activity determines how good you get at the activity. In the language of SIGN, you need to be acutely aware of your *I*s (Instinct), your *G*s (Growth), and your *N*s (Needs), because they drive your *S*s (Success). More simply, your appetites drive your abilities. At least those that last.

Conventional wisdom will tell you something different. It says that what drives your successes is diligent practice. On the surface, at least, this isn't wrong. In fact, recent research into expert performers in fields as diverse as basketball, chess, software design, and Scrabble reveals that, according to the professor who led the twenty-year research study, "there's surprisingly little hard evidence that anyone could achieve any kind of exceptional performance without spending a lot of time perfecting it." The *New York Times* summarized the research thus: "This is not to say all of us have equal potential. Michael Jordan, even if he hadn't spent countless hours in the gym, would still have been a better basketball player than most of us. But without those hours in the gym, he wouldn't have become the player he was."

So yes, conventional wisdom is correct to say that you tend to get good at those activities you practice. But this isn't a terribly significant thing to say—we've heard it, in one form or another, starting with our first T-ball coach. What is significant is that you do not practice all activities with the same degree of effort. Your appetites determine which activities you yearn to practice and which ones you don't. You are drawn in by some activities and repelled by others, and those you are drawn to, you practice more, so you get better, and so you practice more, and so your performance improves still further. Up and up this spirals, with your appetites fueling your practice and your practice driving your performance. Using SIGN language again, the *I* draws you in, the *G* keeps you focused, and the *N* makes you feel great, which in turn fuels the *I*, which draws you back in. Onward and upward it goes, with your appetites driving your abilities.

BUT WHAT ABOUT ACTIVITIES THAT ARE
ALL APPETITE, NO ABILITY?

Yes, what about those activities that you have a yearning to do, but no matter how frequently you practice, and how much fun you have while doing them, and how great you feel when you're done with them, you never seem to get any better? What happens when you feel lots of *I*, *G*, and *N*, but you just can't seem to generate any *S*? What about those all-appetite, no-ability activities?

Well, in common parlance, we have a word for them. We call them *hobbies*. And they stay hobbies because no one is paying you to do them. In hobby world you can indulge your desire to throw oil paint onto a canvas or hack away with your seven iron or fill your shower with song, and no one really cares that your performance is significantly subpar—or, in the case of the seven iron, significantly over par—because your livelihood doesn't depend on your performance.

But back in the real world, the world of work and wages and customers and expectations, we quickly dismiss this as a luxury. Very few of us maintain a strong appetite for an activity in which we clearly have no ability. We often see people expressing a strong appetite for a job or role that carries with it lots of money and prestige, but that's different—here they are yearning for the money and the prestige, not the actual activities of the role.

It's a rare day that you'll see someone pining to do a specific activity at which she is consistently mediocre. It must be something in our DNA. Way back in our prehistory, the person who still yearned to be a tracker even though he had trouble recognizing or even spotting the most obvious spoor would have been the first to be kicked out of the tribe when resources ran low. He wouldn't have survived, and neither would his genes. In the language of evolution, it's not an adaptive trait to continually yearn to do something you are manifestly bad at, and so, although one occasionally runs up against it, it's unlikely to survive in many of us today.

WHO IS THE BEST JUDGE OF YOUR STRENGTHS?

The conventional definition of a strength as an activity you are good at, though intuitively sensible, does great damage to your relationship to your own strengths. It immediately distances you from them. It suggests that you, of all people, cannot be trusted to evaluate exactly what you are good at. And so, from an early age you were trained to look outside of yourself for "objective" assessments of your "true" strengths. At home you were told to look to your parents; at school you looked to your teachers; and at work you turned to your manager or your performance appraisal to confirm or deny what your strengths were.

But if your strengths are those activities that make you feel strong, then the person best qualified to identify them—indeed, the only person qualified to identify them—is you. You don't need a manager or a performance appraisal or even a psychologist to tell you what your strengths are. You may need help spotting the signs last week or capturing your reaction to your activities this week, but so long as you get this help, *you* are the best judge of your strengths. You know which activities draw you back to them time and again. You know which activities you can't help volunteering for. You know which activities keep your interest and your concentration with almost no effort. You know which activities leave you feeling strong, fulfilled, powerful.

If you say you love getting things organized, finding a place for everything and everything in its place, then no one—no boss, no teammate—can tell you you're wrong. No one's assessment trumps yours. Sure, they can tell you that you're not getting things organized in the company-sanctioned way. And, sure, they can tell you that there is a better, more efficient way of getting things organized. They can even tell you that sometimes your need to make things organized gets in the way of serving customers or making a sale or some other such outcome. All this is legitimate performance feedback, and you should keep your mind open to it.

But what no one can do better than you is identify which activities you love and which you loathe. No one can tell you which activities make you feel strong and which ones make you feel weak. Here, your perspective is, and will always be, sure and true. So trust it. Pay close attention to your appetites. Capture them, clarify, and confirm them, and outstanding performance will follow.

CAPTURE, CLARIFY, AND CONFIRM

Learning how to capture, clarify, and confirm your strengths is your goal for this step. You'll learn how to examine the actual activities that fill up your week, look for the telltale signs that point to your strengths, and identify them. More specifically, by the end of the step, you'll be able to write three statements that describe your strengths vividly. These three Strength Statements will not be derived from a personality test or a performance appraisal. Instead they will stem from your pulling apart the jumble of activities filling your week, sorting out the strong from the weak, and then distilling the strong down to the most tangible level possible. (We'll deal with your weaknesses in step four.) These three activities will be you at your most pro-

THE LAST WORD ON STRENGTHS

What does a strength look like?

- It looks like consistent, near-perfect performance.

Which three ingredients combine to create a strength?

1. Talents. Because you are so close to your own talents, they are most effectively measured by personality profiles such as the Clifton StrengthsFinder, Myers-Briggs, and the Kolbe Conative Index. Talents are innate.
2. Skills. Skills are learned.
3. Knowledge. Knowledge is learned.

What does one of your strengths actually feel like to you?

- When you do it, you feel effective—the S of SIGN.
- Before you do it, you actively look forward to it—the I of SIGN.
- While you are doing it, you feel inquisitive and focused—the G of SIGN.
- After you've done it, you feel fulfilled and authentic—the N of SIGN.

So, to identify your own strengths, pay close attention to how specific activities make you feel. Your feelings reveal your strengths.

ductive, innovative, resilient, and focused. They will be you at your best.

To give you a sense of what your Strength Statements might look like, here are my three. As you'll see, for reasons I'll explain a little later, each begins with the phrase "I feel strong when ..."

S **strength** statement card

I feel strong when...

I interview someone who excels at his job and explore why he excels.

S **strength** statement card

I feel strong when...

I present, but only to a large group of people, on a subject I know a lot about, when I'm completely prepared, and when I know my presentation will further a mission.

S **strength** statement card

I feel strong when...

I take the time to study an organization that excels.

In your eyes, these statements may not seem particularly impressive. But to me they are a revelation—a gob-smacking, mind-blowing, "oh-why-didn't-I-think-of-that-before?" revelation. Every time I read them, I am floored. They appear to me so terribly important, so completely and permanently true, the truth of the ages, at once universal and utterly unique. They organize and make sense of the world and my place within it.

Of course, the fact of the matter is that they are neither important nor revelatory to anyone except me. It is always this way. We've helped thousands of people craft their own Strength Statements (you can find more examples below, and at Simply Strengths.com), and although they vary as much as the people do, the best of them all share one characteristic: They all move the person who wrote them. When done right, they reveal to the person something he or she has always known, something fine and specific and true, but which had been drowned out by the demands and general clamor of the adult world. To reclaim them—to capture, clarify, and confirm them—should be a deeply emotional act. The emotion might be joy at what you've rediscovered in yourself, or inspiration to make the most of yourself, or regret at what you've neglected in yourself all these years. But whatever it is, it should be strong.

So if, when you're done with yours and read them for the first time, you feel . . . nothing, cross them out and try again. You're not there yet.

For me—as it will be for you when you craft yours—the emotional punch of these statements lies in their specificity. Early in my career, I found that I loved interviewing people, which, over time, led me into what today would be called a professional coaching role. I would interview various leaders at our client companies, identify their strengths and weaknesses, and then try to coach them to become more effective. It was good work, useful work, both financially and altruistically, and yet I gradually realized that it bored me to no end. I loved interviewing, and so I should have loved this job, but I didn't. And I never would.

The truth, I now realize, is that I don't love interviewing. Instead, and more specifically, I love interviewing people who excel at their job, to discover why they excel. Many of the leaders I interviewed in my coach role did not excel at their job. In fact they were struggling—they were good people, but bad leaders. In my coach role, I was supposed to interview them, study how, where, and if they fit any aspect of their role, and then see if we could maneuver their world so they could engage with it more effectively. I should have loved doing this—there was the intellectual challenge of it, let alone the noble sense of helping another human being—but for no good reason I didn't. Not at all. I have no idea why, but I am at my best—most challenged, creative, uplifted, mentally sharp, helpful, innovative—not when I am interviewing people, but when, and only when, I am interviewing people who excel at their work and explore why they excel. Any other kind of interviewing leaves me cold.

Distilling my Strength Statements down to this level of detail is critical for me. Not just in terms of my emotional well-being but also in terms of my performance. I will make my greatest possible contribution for the longest possible period of time only if I can structure my weeks so that I am deliberately filling my next week with more of these specific activities than I did the week before. If each week I can play to some aspect of these activities—it might be the "seeking out the right person to interview" aspect of number one, or the "preparing the presentation" aspect of number two, or the "taking notes" aspect of number three—I will have an invigorating, creative, and productive week. If I can't, for whatever reason—the demands of my customers, or my colleagues, or my own lack of focus—then I won't.

And the same applies to you.

STRENGTH STATEMENT EXAMPLES

S **strength** statement card

I feel strong when…

I'm coaching my team to meet their quarterly sales goals.

S **strength** statement card

I feel strong when…

COLLABORATING WITH OTHERS TO DEVELOP CONTENT FOR OUR NEW SERVICE OFFERINGS

S **strength** statement card

I feel strong when…

I AM DESIGNING POWERFUL CONVERSATIONS TO HELP PEOPLE HAVE THE IMPACT THEY INTEND.

S | **strength** statement card

I feel strong when...

LEADING OR PARTICIPATING IN
BRAINSTORMING SESSIONS TO COME
UP WITH ENGINEERING SOLUTIONS
TO COMPLEX DESIGN CHALLENGES.

S | **strength** statement card

I feel strong when...

I synthesize and compile
Information into a clear
report.

Your challenge in the months and years to come can be summed up in the question "How can I play to my strengths a little more this week than I did last week?" As such, you must begin by carving three Strength Statements that are precise, distinct, specific, and blow you away every time you read them.

• • •

The most effective way to identify your strengths is through a simple three-phase process. This process won't require you to step back and away from your work. Instead it will ask you to pay attention to your work more closely than ever before and to sort out exactly how the things you do make you feel.

This process begins with the challenge of *capturing* which specific activities over the course of a week played to your strengths and which ones played to your weaknesses. This phase is critical. If you don't do it, you won't have the raw material you need to craft Strength Statements that are powerful, vivid, and true.

Next you need to *clarify* the specific activities you've captured and arrive at statements that are both precise enough to preserve the original emotional punch and general enough for you to apply each week. (Look back at my three, and you'll see what I mean by "precise and generalizable.")

Finally, you'll want to *confirm* that these three are indeed your most dominant strengths. To help you, at the end of this step you'll find a Strengths Test. Run each statement through this test, and you'll discover whether these are indeed three activities that should dominate your time and attention at work.

Capture

At this point, if you were going through one of our strengths courses, we would give you a small pad, called a reMEMO pad, made up half of green pages and half of red. Since we can't actually give you the reMEMO pad itself, we've taken from it twenty red pages and twenty green and included them in the back of this book. Turn to the back, and you'll see that on the green pages is written "I Loved It," and on the red pages, predictably, "I Loathed It." Carry the book around with you next week, and whenever you find yourself doing something that makes you feel one of the following, scribble down the activity on one of the green sheets:

Powerful

Confident

Natural

Smooth

On fire

High

"I've got this wired."

Great

Authentic

"That was easy."

Awesome

"When can I do this again?"

The moment you feel any one of these emotions, open the book to the green pages and write down exactly what you're doing. Don't wait till the end of the day, or worse yet, the end of the week, because you won't remember the specific detail of what you were doing. The instant you become aware of a significantly positive feeling—assuming you're not in the middle of a conversation—open the book and capture what you're doing. Then put it away and get on with your day.

Likewise, if during the course of the week, you find yourself feeling one of the following, write down on one of the red pages exactly what you are doing:

Drained

"Time's going by so slowly."

"I can't concentrate."

Frustrated

Wiped out

Forced

"I'm getting a migraine."

"How much longer?!"

Irritated

Bored

"Why can't the new guy do this?"

If you want to add a grumpy face or a downward arrow or a big flag, fine. Use whatever pictures you need to capture the emotion of the moment. But whatever you do, be sure to write exactly what you were doing when you felt this negative charge.

On the accompanying page, you'll see a guide to prime you for what you should be feeling when you scribble on the green pages versus the red pages. Of course, there will be many activities that are, in effect, neutral, and that prompt no scribbling from you at all. Don't push yourself to write down something after every activity. Wait until what you're doing forces your hand.

To help you get started, on the following page you'll find a couple of examples of the activities that others have written down during the course of their week. Take a look at these and then set about your week, capturing as you go.

At the end of your week, tear out the green pages you've written on—save the red pages for step four—and spread them out over a flat surface. Then sort them into a pile, with the most positive pages on top, all the way down to the least positive

	When I am **doing** an activity the *strengthens* me	When I am **doing** an activity the *weakens* me
I am thinking…	☐ "I can't wait to start!" ☐ "This is fun!" ☐ "I could do this forever." ☐ "This is my calling." ☐ "This is perfect for me." ☐ "Just try and stop me."	☐ "I hate it when I have to do this." ☐ "Will this ever end?" ☐ "This is going to take forever." ☐ "Thank goodness this is nearly over." ☐ "Can I sit this one out?"
I am feeling…	☐ Powerful, Passionate ☐ Euphoric, Enthusiastic ☐ Natural, Authentic ☐ Smooth, Confident	☐ Frustrated, Fragmented ☐ Disjointed, Awkward ☐ Drained, Despondent ☐ Bored, Distracted
I want to…	☐ Find a way to do more of it. ☐ Learn more about it. ☐ Find role models and people that I can learn from. ☐ Look for people that are really good at it.	☐ Avoid having to do it again. ☐ Get the new guy to do it. ☐ Shove it to the right side of my desk and ignore it. ☐ Do anything else instead.

pages on the bottom. Then "deal" off the top of your deck your top three green pages and lay them out in front of you.

These three specific activities provide the raw material for

I *Loved* It

I *Loved* It

I felt strong when...

I renegotiated a contract with David Jones's company for another four years.

I *Loved* It

I felt strong when...

I met with my team and discussed our business plan and goals for this quarter. I really love hearing people's ideas on how to reach our goals.

I *Loved* It

I felt strong when...

I came up with a great email marketing campaign to promote a new product for angel food services.

I *Loathed* It

I *Loathed* It

I felt weak (drained, bored) when...

I had to listen to Sally Gordon complain about equipment that was not working in her store.

I *Loathed* It

I felt weak (drained, bored) when...

I talked to Veronica about her snappy attitude and negative body language during our meeting with Dan. I hate confrontation!

I *Loathed* It

I felt weak (drained, bored) when...

I had to manually enter client names and contact information in our database. It's so monotonous!

your three Strength Statements™. Study them. You're now going to turn these three specific activities in the past—"I loved it when . . ."—into three Strength Statements™ expressed in the present: "I feel strong when . . ."

Clarify

My week yielded three activities. On one card I'd written, "I interviewed Rosa—interesting lady." Rosa was the director of housekeeping for the Hampton Inn at Los Angeles International Airport. She managed thirteen housekeepers, and by any measure—guest satisfaction scores, employee retention, lost work days—she was brilliant at it.

On another I'd written, "Preparing for the presentation to the Chick-fil-A group." That week I had prepared for a presentation to a large group of Chick-fil-A restaurant operators. I hadn't given it yet. I'd just prepared for it. But it seemed to me like some of the strength signs were there while I was preparing.

And third, I had researched and read a series of articles about the New Zealand rugby team. This team, called the All Blacks because of the color of their uniform, are a mystery. Despite hailing from a relatively small nation—there are twelve times more sheep (fifty million) than New Zealanders (four million)—the All Blacks are, and have been for over a century, the most successful professional sporting team in the world, with a century-long winning percentage of .733.

In and of itself, capturing these activities was a useful exercise because, as we've just learned, these three activities are strengths of mine. However, as they stand, these activities are too specific to be useful to me week in and week out. Obviously,

I don't need to be interviewing Rosa each week or reading up on the All Blacks.

Since I will be most effective only if I can deliberately push my time at work toward my strengths, what I need is a description of my strengths that is specific enough to make it clear—to me, my colleagues, and my manager—where I should spend more of my time. Which new skills should I learn? Which projects should I seek out? And so on. Yet the description should be generic enough for me to apply it to the changing circumstances of each week. In short, I need to clarify the essence of each of my top three green pages while not losing entirely their specificity.

To do this, you must first change the tense of your statement from the past ("I loved it when . . .") to the present ("I feel strong when . . ."). This is easily done.

Second, you must identify exactly which aspects of the activity are critical and must be preserved if the activity is to generate in you the same positive emotions in future weeks as it obviously did this week. If this sounds like an exercise in subtle self-analysis, take heart. You don't need a trained psychologist to subject the activity to some kind of psychological centrifuge. All you need to do, with each of your top green pages, is ask yourself four simple "Does it matter . . . ?" questions:

1. Does it matter *why* I do this activity?
2. Does it matter *who* I do this activity with/to/for?
3. Does it matter *when* I am doing this activity?
4. Does it matter *what* this activity is about?

Using these four questions, you'll quickly discover which aspects of the activity really matter and therefore absolutely must be present if they are to make you feel strong week after week; and conversely, which aspects of the activity are largely irrelevant and can be ignored.

For example, if I run my first green page—"I loved it when . . . I interviewed Rosa"—through these questions, this is what I get:

Q. Does it matter why I am doing this activity?
A. No. I could be doing the interview as part of a book research project, or to prepare for a presentation, or to help Rosa become even more effective. It wouldn't matter. Any one of them makes me feel strong.

Q. Does it matter who I do this activity with/to/for?
A. Yes. I only seem to like interviewing people who excel at their work. No idea why, but there it is.

Q. Does it matter when I do this activity?
A. No. It doesn't matter if this happens at the beginning of my day, or the end, at the beginning of a research project or in the middle; it always makes me feel strong. It's always something I look forward to.

Q. Does it matter what this activity is about?
A. Yes. If I interviewed Rosa about her relationships at work, or her career aspirations, or her political beliefs, it wouldn't strengthen me at all. I only feel strong when I am interviewing her about why she excels in her role.

So, putting these answers together, I can go from a green page on which I scribbled, "I loved it when interviewed Rosa" to a carefully crafted Strength Statement that reads:

(S) **strength** statement card

I feel strong when...

> I interview someone who excels at
> his job and explore why he excels.

Now, at last, I have arrived at an insight into my strengths that is at once emotionally resonant and deeply affirming, but still gives me practical guidance about what I should do more of next week.

In case you are still a bit unclear about how to make the transition from green page to Strength Statement, here's a more advanced example. On my second green page I'd written, "I loved it when I was preparing for my presentation to Chick-fil-A's operators." Subjecting this green page to those four "Does it matter . . . ?" questions, this is what I got:

Q. **Does it matter why I am doing this activity?**
A. Yes, for two reasons. First, because I don't like preparing just for the sake of organizing my thoughts. I seem to get excited about preparing only if the result of the preparation is going to be some kind of presentation. Preparation without presentation holds no joy for me. Second, both the preparation and the presentation had better be part of some larger project or mission. If I am preparing for the sake of giving a one-off speech, it starts to bug me. Right or wrong, it weakens me to think of myself as merely entertainment.

Q. Does it matter who I do this activity with/to/for?
A. Yes and no. No, in the sense that I don't care who the audience is. I have stood up in front of a room full of pediatricians and one full of juvenile offenders, and both invigorated me. But, yes, it matters "who I do this activity to" in the sense that the larger the audience is, the more invigorated I am. Preparing for a presentation to six people somehow both scares and bores me. Multiply that number by a thousand, and suddenly I'm energized.

Q. Does it matter when I am doing this activity?
A. No. As with my first green page, it doesn't matter when I do my preparing. It could be on a plane or in the library; 8:00 in the morning or 11:00 at night; under the tightest of deadlines or with months to spare. I always feel strong when I am thinking through a presentation.

Q. Does it matter what this activity is about?
A. Yes. I am drained by the activity of preparing for a brand-new presentation, just as I am drained by giving it. Some people like starting things from scratch. Not me. I am depleted by the very idea of starting from scratch, researching from scratch, presenting from scratch. The brand new, the green field, the "never-been-there-before" might invigorate you, but it intimidates me. I am at my strongest only when my preparation and presentation involve taking a subject I already know a great deal about and extending this knowledge still further. At heart, I am a hedgehog—"know a lot about a little"—not a fox.

These answers combine to transform the green page "I loved it when . . . I was preparing for my presentation to Chick-fil-A's operators" into this Strength Statement:

> ## ⓢ strength statement card
>
> **I feel strong when…**
>
> I present, but only to a large group of people, on a subject I know a lot about, when I'm completely prepared, and when I know my presentation will further a mission.

As I described earlier, this statement might seem common-place to you, but to me it is powerfully clarifying. It both reveals where my strength and power reside and shows me what kinds of activities must always be present for my weeks at work to be most effective. It's a gift.

Take one of your top three green pages and ask yourself those "Does it matter . . . ? " questions, then write your Strength Statement. When you're satisfied with one, repeat the process with green pages two and three.

You should now have three statements, derived from a regular week at work, that vividly capture activities that make you feel strong. Take a long look at them. Simply put, your goal for this coming year will be to figure out how to exploit each of these a little more effectively week after week after week.

Confirm

Before you launch into exactly how to do that—how to explain to your colleagues what you're doing, how to persuade your boss to help you, how to stay on your strengths track despite other people's sometimes well-meaning attempts to pull you off—you should subject your three statements to the Strengths Test below.

Strengths Test™

Look for **SIGNs** of a strength

On a scale of 1–5, 1 = *strongly disagree* and 5 = *strongly agree*, write down your responses to the following statements:

S = SUCCESS

1. I have been tremendously successful at this type of activity.   1 2 3 4 5

2. Other people often tell me I have a gift for this type of activity.   1 2 3 4 5

3. I have been given prizes or recognition for doing this type of activity.   1 2 3 4 5

I = INSTINCT

4. I do this type of activity every day.   1 2 3 4 5

5. I often find myself volunteering for this type of activity.   1 2 3 4 5

6. This type of activity is a "gut reaction" to me.   1 2 3 4 5

G = GROWTH

7. I pick up this type of activity quickly.   1 2 3 4 5

8. I find myself thinking about this type of activity every day.   1 2 3 4 5

9. I can't wait to learn new techniques for doing this activity.   1 2 3 4 5

N = NEEDS

10. I always look forward to doing this type of activity.   1 2 3 4 5

11. It's fun for me to think back to when I was doing this type of activity.   1 2 3 4 5

12. Doing this type of activity is one of my greatest personal satisfactions.   1 2 3 4 5

People might not trust you to assess accurately how good you are at something, but you can certainly be trusted to judge your own emotions. This test asks you to rate your emotions in a few key areas. Your ratings will allow you to confirm, or, on the flip side, cause you to question, that each of your Strength Statements is indeed a strength.

Start with your first statement, then run the next two through it. (At SimplyStrengths.com, you'll find an electronic version to print out if you don't want to mark up the test in the book.)

Look for a score of 53 or above. Any activity scoring at this level or higher not only fires in you the right kind of powerful emotions, but you've obviously focused on learning and applying it to such an extent that others have recognized your successes. A score of 53 or above is a true strength. It is a source of competitive advantage for you and must serve as a focus for the weeks and months ahead.

What about an activity that scores 46 to 52? Should you discard it and go back to your green cards to find some other activity? Well, it depends on which questions brought down the score. If you rated the first three questions low, while the *I, G,* and *N* questions got high marks, it's a sign that this is indeed a strength but one that you have yet to apply effectively. Your appetites are strong, but you have yet to translate them into the kind of performance that would command the attention of colleagues and managers. So stay focused on this activity, discipline yourself to seek out the necessary skills and knowledge, keep practicing, and quite soon you should see your performance start to get attention.

By contrast, if your answers to questions four through twelve pulled down the score, then the chances are that it's not a strength. It lacks the urgency and the extreme positive reactions so characteristic of a strength. So look closely at the activity. Why couldn't you mark 5, "strongly agree," to many of the questions? Perhaps you didn't clarify the activity quite right. Perhaps you left out one crucial element in your Strength Statement, an element that, if included, would have jumped some of your scores from a 4 to a 5. Before you discard the activity and go all the way back to your green pages, consider the possibility that one small detail was left out. Go back and find it, and then run the statement through the test once more.

If an activity scored below 46, it's highly unlikely to be a strength. In which case, how did it wind up on your green pages? Well, perhaps last week wasn't typical for you. Perhaps you were at a conference or were preparing for a one-off presentation or meeting. If this is the reason, then repeat the capture phase and see whether, during a regular week, different activities end up on your green pages. Then clarify and confirm them and see what scores you get.

If your last two weeks were generally typical of your weeks at work, and you still netted activities that didn't score higher than 46, you may have a bigger problem. You may be in the wrong role. In fact, when a week goes by with you paying close attention to how your specific activities make you feel, and you find nothing that prompts you to mark 5s on the Strengths Test, alarm bells should start ringing. There may be good reasons why you're in this role—it was your only option at the time, it will serve as a stepladder to some other role, it pays well—but rest assured, without activities to invigorate you, you won't be very effective, creative, or resilient, at least not for long. Take your appetites seriously and start planning your exit.

Will Your Strength Statements Stay the Same Year after Year?

No. As we described in the previous step, the most dominant themes of your personality—the talent themes measured by the Clifton StrengthsFinder, for example—will indeed remain consistent across time and situations. But these talents will manifest themselves differently according to the particular circumstances you're facing.

For example, one of my top five themes is Ideation, a craving to find the core concepts that can explain the most events. Research on the Clifton StrengthsFinder strongly suggests that I will always be this way; that no matter what my circumstances are, I will always find myself digging beneath the surface, looking for the causes. However, the strengths created by this theme will undoubtedly vary over time.

Early in my career, I was involved in designing preemployment interviews to select candidates for jobs. I can still recall how much I loved the activity of sorting through the transcripts of focus groups and searching for clues to questions for my interviews. Back then, if I had put myself through this capture-clarify-confirm process, I know one of my Strength Statements would have read: "I feel strong when I pore over transcripts looking for the perfect questions." Today, as you've seen, my Strength Statements read rather differently.

This difference reflects not that I've changed my personality, but that, over the course of my career, I have remained inquisitive, and this inquisitiveness has led to new opportunities and new roles—some of which worked out great, some of which didn't. This whole body of experience has been fed into my system, been metabolized in some way, and created in me strengths—activities that make me feel strong—that are related but different from ten years ago.

The same will apply to you. The core aspects of your personality will remain the same. But, over the years, the world will press in upon you, and you will be asked to take on new responsibilities, or you will press in upon the world and demand new experiences and new challenges, and you will soak up all this and try to make some sense of it.

The danger, of course, is that you will become confused about where your strengths lie, that you will allow your weeks to fill with activities that do not invigorate you, and that you will, over time, become increasingly unclear about which activities should anchor your weeks at work.

HOW CAN PROFILES SUCH AS THE CLIFTON STRENGTHSFINDER, MYERS-BRIGGS, OR KOLBE HELP YOU IDENTIFY YOUR STRENGTHS?

- These profiles give you a way to step back from yourself and identify your recurring talents, such as competitiveness, or what-if thinking, or altruism. As such, when you capture which specific activities make you feel strong and which don't, these profiles can cue you where to look.

- Review your results before your capture phase, and you will prepare your mind. You will start to think about how you engage with your world and the people within it.

- However, remember: The most direct way to identify your strengths is always to pay attention to how specific activities make you feel. No one can do this better than you. You don't need to take a personality profile to do this. You just need to know how to capture, clarify, and confirm.

- In the search for your strengths, personality-profile results are an intriguing but interim step.

To combat this danger, you should go through the process you just learned—capture-clarify-confirm—twice a year. Pick a week and capture your emotional reactions to the activities of your week, then clarify and confirm what you captured. To seize control of your time at work, you have to know what your targets are, what you want to push your time toward. This twice-a-year process will set your targets.

Fill out the cards provided below, or log onto Simply Strengths.com to complete an electronic version. You can then print them out and keep them front and center on your desk, on your wall, or in your top drawer. Whatever you choose to do

(S) strength statement card

I feel strong when...

(S) strength statement card

I feel strong when...

(S) **strength** statement card

I feel strong when...

with these statements, take them seriously. Elevate them. Spotlight them. Keep them directly in your line of sight.

HEIDI GETS CLEAR

When Heidi went through this capture-clarify-confirm process, she made a disconcerting discovery: Her week yielded far more red pages than green. Spread out on the desk in front of her was the explanation for her malaise, why every day she dreaded tomorrow. She still loved the big things in her job: the Hampton brand, the mission of the hospitality business, the relationships with her colleagues and her boss. What she loathed were the little things: the hourly chasing of hotel managers who wouldn't sign up for the right programs; the arguments with managers who didn't believe in the Hampton 100 percent satisfaction guarantee.

Strangely, as she sat staring at the pile of reds, she realized that the sight of them comforted her. The red pages were a sign that she wasn't burning out on her job and her company. She was simply doing the wrong stuff—a lot of it. Here was the tangible evidence that her week had filled up with the wrong kind of activities, and so here also was the proof that she couldn't work her way out of her rut by putting in more hours. More hours would simply mean more red pages.

Digging beneath the reds, she picked up her few green pages and read what she'd written. It was good to look at her week this way and see on the pages the flashes of her at her best. Lately it had felt that her weeks at work were devoid of them. But, no, here they were, written in her own hand, showing her the way forward.

She pushed the red pages to one side and sorted through the greens. After some shuffling, she found three forcing their way to the top of the miniature deck:

"Visited with Buffalo Hotel group. Their room denials way down. Awesome."

"Taught the new GM class again. Loved it."

"Talked to John about his breakfast setup. Good guy, great ideas."

Heidi subjected each of these to the "Does it matter . . . ?" question. After some back-and-forthing with herself, she landed on these three carefully worded Strength Statements:

S | **strength** statement card

I feel strong when...

I see team members take my ideas and make them their own.

S | **strength** statement card

I feel strong when...

I get to know general managers and owners really well.

Rereading the statements, Heidi didn't struggle to know what she meant or wonder to herself in exactly what situations they would or would not apply, the way one sometimes does with the results from personality tests. Because these statements were derived from her own emotions during a regular workweek, she knew precisely what she was referring to: which hotel managers she had in mind, which particular ideas she had shared with her colleagues and how they had improved on them, which owners she knew well, how long she'd known them, when she'd met them, when they'd joined Hampton, why they'd joined.

These statements seemed to her as inevitable and as deeply familiar as the rooms of the house she grew up in, or the lefts and rights of her daily walk to high school. Over the last few years she hadn't forgotten them, not exactly. Instead it was as if, nudged by the mild hand of this person's needs and that person's needs, she had pushed them each week farther and farther over to the side of her desk until, finally, they'd fallen off and fluttered away.

By writing them out, she had, in effect, reached down, gathered them up, and set them back on the desk in front of her.

Now she sat there staring at them, wondering how she could make them the core of her job.

For a video challenge from me about Step 2, visit Simply Strengths.com.

STEP 3

FREE YOUR STRENGTHS

"HOW CAN YOU MAKE THE MOST OF WHAT STRENGTHENS YOU?"

By now I hope you have captured, clarified, and confirmed three Strength Statements. If you have, and if you've done it right, your world should now be changed. No more vague resentments about your boss or your company. No more excuses or procrastinations. You look at your three Strength Statements, and you know where your power lies. You know that if you could just put these strengths into play, you would contribute more and tolerate more and support more and create more. When the world yanks and tugs at you, and pulls and twists you, you know these strengths will keep you focused, front and center. You look at your Strength Statements, and you know where the steel is.

If you're like most of us, you're probably a little annoyed right now. You're annoyed that over the years you've let the demands and obstacles of your world muffle these strengths. And maybe you're frustrated—with yourself, for not seeing sooner the forces inside you; or with others, for not showing you where you were strong or for deliberately distracting you from your strengths.

And so you want to act. You're rightly impatient. You've been working so hard lately, but not at the right things. At least not enough of the right things. You look at your Strength Statements, and you know you could exert more control over your time at work. You know you could be more rigorous and disciplined about where you choose to spend your minutes. For you it would simply be a question of changing a meeting, or a schedule, or making this phone call, not that one, or spending more time with this person, not that one. It's not going to be that hard. You know it. You want to start now.

If this is how you are feeling, you are just where you need to be: excited, anxious to begin, even a little angry. And, of course, the wonderful thing about the actions you are contemplating right now is that they are not alien to you. They will not demand of you the kind of energy-sapping discipline required when you are forced to do something that doesn't come naturally—the beaming smile for the introvert, the organized calendar for the congenitally disorganized. To free your strengths will require you to do more of precisely those things that do come naturally to you. In fact one of the defining criteria when you selected your strengths was that they came naturally to you. Now all you need to do is release some of that pent-up energy. You're thinking that it should be easy, effortless.

This is to the good. Accept all these emotions, nurse them even, as you strive to seize back some of the control of your time at work. But of course actually taking control will be more difficult. There are powerful forces pulling your week away from your strengths: the needs of your customers, the demands of your colleagues, the expectations of your boss, your own career aspirations. It will take a rare concentration of the mind to push back these forces, channel them, and thereby restore them to their proper place and influence in your time at work.

These forces won't ever disappear completely, nor should they. In fact the key question for you is "How can I use my strengths precisely to fulfill my customers' needs, to listen to the demands of my colleagues, to meet or renegotiate the expectations of my boss, and to honor my career aspirations?" Your answers to these questions will certainly not sap your energy, but neither will they be smooth sailing. The world out there is, at best, indifferent to you and your strengths.

The most extreme answer is that the only way for you to free your strengths is for you to leave your current role or get out from under your misguided boss. In some circumstances, that is the right strategy. But it is the *fifth* possible course of action. There are four distinct strategies you must consider first:

1. Identify exactly how and where each strength helps you in your current role.
2. Find the missed opportunities to leverage each strength in your current role.
3. Learn new skills and techniques to sharpen each strength.
4. Build your job toward each strength.

Later in this step, you'll challenge yourself to pursue each of these strategies, and using something that I call the FREE interview, you'll push yourself to come up with specific things you can do to capitalize on your strengths a little more this week than you did last week. If after giving yourself these four chances, you still feel leaving your role is the only answer, then so be it. And do it.

Just remember, leaving should be your last option, not your first.

Before you get to these strategies, let's return for a moment to Heidi. Her experience in getting weak and getting strong will not mirror yours, of course. But it will be instructive. Read her story and look for the parallels to your own situation. Heidi won't temper your enthusiasm. She'll inform it.

HOW HEIDI GOT WEAK

To appreciate fully how easy it is to fall off one's strengths path, we need to see where it began. Heidi started her career at

Hampton hotels nineteen years ago as a desk clerk while she was still in college. After graduating, she accepted a job as an assistant manager, and a year later, she was made general manager of the Hampton Inn San Antonio/Six Flags. In this role, she flourished. The activities she was asked to perform every day—from making sure that the area where complimentary breakfasts were served was well presented and hospitable, to managing her staff's varying personalities, to spending time greeting guests at check-in time—made her feel strong and fulfilled.

Heidi's success as a GM caught the attention of Hampton headquarters, and, as always seems to happen, she was offered a promotion up, out, and away from the front line. The new job, in the auditing department, certainly appealed to her. Heidi had studied accounting in college and thought that, while she loved the constant activity of running a hotel, maybe she should put her education to a focused, practical use. Plus, she was ambitious.

Heidi's Excel fluency and her intimate understanding of how an individual Hampton hotel actually works were again quickly recognized, and she was soon promoted to a financial analyst in the company's accounting department.

So far, so very typical. A smart, driven employee puts in her time on the front line and then is given the chance to combine this real-world experience with her formal education. Something very similar may have happened to you. Or will.

Heidi now experienced her first career setback, as you probably will at some point in your career. (There the similarities end, since, as you'll see, Heidi's response to it was unorthodox.) Once the excitement of the new role had tailed off, and she came to experience the day-to-day reality of it, something inside of her rang hollow. She was staring at spreadsheets all day, poring over charts and figures, making them line up and match up and even out. She was certainly capable of doing this, but she realized that she missed the interaction she used to have with her employees and customers. Heidi yearned for relationships; she was the kind of GM who knew the personal lives of each of the people working for her, and who would even become friends with her most regular guests. As the weeks dragged by without any outlet for this yearning, she felt a vague but strong need to act.

So Heidi, the senior financial analyst on the fast track to bigger things, took a part-time job as a customer-service representative at Bed Bath & Beyond. She put on her uniform and her headset, and showed up at 7:30 a.m. on Saturdays and Sundays ready for a day in the retail trenches.

Ask her about it today, and she'll joke that she "did it for the discount." But push her a little harder, and she reveals that the financial compensation had nothing to do with why she needed to get a second job. The real reason, of course, is that Heidi felt a void in her life when she cut herself off from the regular interaction with a variety of people. While Heidi didn't yet know the techniques to get clear about what exactly she loved about engaging with others (as she did when she wrote her Strength Statements), the instinctual force of her strengths was pushing her nonetheless.

Was getting a job at Bed Bath & Beyond a smart solution for Heidi? Not really. Remember, Heidi doesn't feel strong when she's generically interacting with people (though in a general sense, she can't live without it either). Heidi feels strong:

- when she helps a hotel manager take a good hotel, or hotel group, and makes it #1;
- when people take her ideas and make them their own;

- when she gets to know the GMs and owners she works with really well.

The customer service rep role didn't allow her to play to any of these strengths. Yes, she was meeting people every day, lots and lots of people. But what she was actually being paid to do every day was to solve these people's problems. She was not being paid to help someone go from above average to excellent, nor to share her ideas for better ways of doing things, nor even to build relationships. Once she got off the phone with a customer who was wondering where his louvered blinds were, that was it. The customer was gone.

The power of Heidi's strengths lies in their specificity, as it does with yours. Her customer service role certainly met the people-interaction element of her Strength Statements, but precious little else. Her reaching for this role turned out to be a desperate but ultimately misguided cry for help, a flare shot into a cloudy night's sky.

There's a lesson here: If you want to become one of the two out of ten who plays to their strengths most of the time, don't move yourself into a role that is close to but not actually in your strengths zone, no matter how powerful your urge to do so. It will soon frustrate you. Or if your current situation is so awful that you have to move somewhere, anywhere, know that this close-to-but-not-quite-there role will offer you only a temporary respite.

Heidi's flare soon burned out, and though she didn't have the words to describe exactly what was missing, she knew her emptiness wouldn't be filled by a headset at Bed Bath & Beyond. She ended her moonlighting stint, returned her full attention to Hampton, and, after hearing of an opening for a brand director, actively sought out the position. It seemed like the perfect job in that it put her in a position where she was a point person for building relationships, sharing ideas, and providing support. In addition, it would allow her to use her double knowledge: the firsthand operational side of the hotel business run by the owners and their GMs, and also the nuts-and-bolts program and performance requirements set by Hampton corporate in which she had become fluent during her time at headquarters. Heidi thought that maybe all her roles leading up to this job represented her "dues." She certainly felt like she'd paid them. If you'd met Heidi when she took over her new position, you would have recognized a young woman energized and excited about her future.

Unfortunately, this feeling lasted little more than a year. At the time, the role of Hampton brand directors was designed so that the majority of their time was spent trying to revive the worst-performing Hampton hotels. And typically, the worst-performing hotels became so for a few blatant reasons: They ignored strategic companywide directives from the corporate parent, they had apathetic management, and they ignored brand directors who tried to help them.

So here was Heidi chasing all of these struggling hotels, helping them grow from bad to below average, sharing ideas with people who didn't want them, and attempting to build relationships with people who mostly didn't even want to take her call. And she was miserable.

To you, from the vantage point of knowing her three Strength Statements, her predicament must seem obvious; almost absurd. "Well, no wonder she's frustrated! She's got herself into a role that doesn't give her a chance to express her strengths."

But put yourself in her shoes for a moment. Heidi hadn't yet captured, clarified, and confirmed her strengths. She was just doing her job every day, a job she'd actively campaigned for. She was doing her best at it, and her best was pretty good. Yet, for some unfathomable reason, she wasn't looking forward to doing it again tomorrow. From her vantage point, with her nose pressed up close against the wall of weekly stuff to get done, the solution was far from obvious.

Not least because her feelings weren't all negative. Because of the conventional wisdom that if something comes easy to us, then the activity isn't as valuable as those we struggle with, we actually admire people who "put up with it." We even make heroes of people who "work through it," people who, like Heidi, build up a different kind of strength: the strength of tolerance.

On any given day, then, Heidi didn't know quite what to think.

One day, buoyed by the conventional wisdom, she'd say to herself, "Stop moaning and just put up with it, and people will thank me for it."

The very next day, she'd wonder whether the perfect job she thought she would love, that seemed to have all the right components to play to her generalized sense of her strengths, was just a figment of her overly optimistic imagination.

And the next day, she'd think that maybe she should quit the company she'd dedicated her entire professional career to.

And on particularly bad days, she'd conclude that maybe there was nothing wrong with the job at all; maybe there was something wrong with her.

This is where we met her at the beginning of the book. Driven, dissatisfied with mediocrity, business savvy, experienced, ambitious—and burned out.

HOW HEIDI GOT STRONG

The way out of her malaise became clear with one insight and one phone call.

The insight was this: The job itself wasn't stopping Heidi from doing what she loved. The job she loved was there, it was just camouflaged beneath activities she loathed. If she could change the activities, she could change her life.

So she captured, clarified, and confirmed her strengths. Then, one Monday morning, she sat down at her desk, pulled out her first Strength Statement, and thought about it.

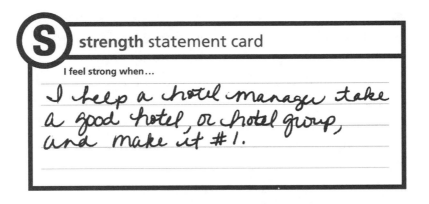

It gave her a shiver to think how different this approach was from how she'd been doing her job for the last few years. But rather than dwelling on the radical nature of what she was about to do, she reached for the Hampton weekly report detailing how each hotel she was responsible for had performed the previous week. Instead of scouring the bottom half of the report as she normally would have, she started from the top and began looking at how her best hotels were doing.

It wasn't easy—the lure of years of habit kept pulling her eyes downward—but Heidi made a secret deal with herself. She would concentrate only on the hotels in the upper third, hotels that were doing well but could still use some attention in a particular area.

Flipping through the report, Heidi came across a hotel that was excelling in many areas, such as revenue per available room, occupancy rates, and guest satisfaction scores. But for some reason, it had tremendously high "usable denials." In Hampton parlance, this means that there are guests who want to book multiple-night stays at a hotel but can't because the hotel is sold out for one of the evenings the guest wanted. Any usable denial is intensely frustrating for GMs because it means they are forced to turn away prime, multinight-stay guests.

For Heidi, the sight of this particular hotel, with its distinctive pattern of overall excellence combined with one area of "opportunity," was immediately intriguing. Here was a solid hotel that, with a little help from her, could become a Hampton award winner. Heidi knew that Hampton had a number of protocols and programs that could be used to prevent usable denials from happening, such as establishing two-night minimums for certain nights of the week or holding a set number of rooms for multiple-night stays. Of course, just because Heidi knew this, it didn't mean that each of the GMs did.

So Heidi called the hotel, asked to speak to the GM, breezed through the small talk, and quickly brought up the subject of the sky-high denial rate. She was ready, as she always was, to parry the inevitable defensiveness with a quick list of suggested actions, but she needn't have bothered. There was no defensiveness.

"They were so happy that I called and genuinely wanted to talk with me about the problem," says Heidi. "The GM was already aware of the usable denials and was wrestling with how to solve it." Heidi was so used to getting the runaround from managers who just hoped their problems would go away, or who saw calls from her as authoritative meddling from the corporate parent, that she was momentarily nonplussed.

Here was a hotel GM who actually wanted her help, who kept her on the phone as they debated possible solutions, who invited her to come visit the hotel the following month to continue the discussion, and who, when the call was finally over, actually went ahead and implemented the plans they agreed on.

It didn't hurt that the GM's bonus was based on the hotel's revenue performance, but so much the better. This financial element just furthered the win-win-win nature of the solution. The GM got something he wanted, Hampton increased its revenue and kept its guests happy, and these measurable increases also helped Heidi justify the attention she was giving the hotel.

"In the next report I could see that the changes were working because their number of denials went down and their revenues went up. Coming from an accounting/finance background, I like to have concrete numbers to prove this was working." It would also come in handy if her boss questioned her new approach.

The experience she had on this one call caused her to rethink how the hotels she was responsible for perceived her. Heidi liked the fact that this hotel GM saw her as more of a partner or a consultant than an authority figure who was brought in to discipline a poorly performing asset. She liked the feeling she got when she thought of herself in this new role. Excited by the experience, she vowed that from this point on she would ditch as much as she could the role of corporate babysitter dealing with adolescent hotels that didn't really want to get their business together, and instead work only with those hotels who really wanted to win. Her vow sounded like this:

"Each day I will call one hotel in my upper third and find

some way it can increase its overall performance. One call per day. This is where I'll start."

And she did. And with this one specific commitment, she started a gradual but significant shift in how she spent her time at work. Each of these consulting calls led to another followup call, a more positive kind of call; and then to a different kind of meeting with the GM or owner; and then to a different conversation with her boss, and with her colleagues; and then to a different, better set of performance outcomes; and a different set of emotional outcomes. Not always better, not in every case, but mostly so, one activity after another, every day moving her further away from the old job, and closer and closer to the same job, doing very different stuff.

We'll learn about some of these actions and outcomes in the next steps. How did Heidi deal with the lower-performing hotels? How did she manage to stop doing some of the activities that dragged her down? How did she persuade her boss and colleagues to get on board with her? For now, just know that her trajectory toward sustained high performance began with one commitment to one specific action, then it rippled out from there. So will yours.

YOUR STRONG WEEK PLAN

For most of us, the challenge is similar to Heidi's. Like her, we do not need to seek out an utterly different role. Rather, all we need to do is find those activities at work that do indeed play to our strengths and then fill most of our time with them. As we said in the introduction, we need to turn the *best* of our job into *most* of our job.

To make this happen, you will need to establish in your life a specific routine or regimen that is straightforward enough for you to do regularly but meaty enough to keep your time at work centered on and moving continually toward your strengths. You don't need this routine because, lacking it, your strengths would shut off and stop working for you—as you know by now, your strengths represent a constant and irrepressible force that demands expression. You need it because the world at large cannot be trusted to channel this force for you. The world is not concerned with you and your strengths and is as likely to encourage you to let your strengths run free as it is to place obstacles in your way; or tempt you down the wrong paths, paths that lead to confusion, frustration, Bed Bath & Beyond.

The most effective routine is a Strong Week Plan.

There's magic in the seven days of a week. When you are asked to plan for next year, you may manage to define a few carefully calibrated goals: what you will get done. But you rarely take it down to the level of specific activities: what you will actually be doing. Even a month is too long a time frame to wrap your head around. Whereas, at the other extreme, days, hours, and minutes are too disjointed to provide you any real momentum.

Only a week strikes the perfect practical and psychological note. If I ask you to describe a strong week, you won't talk about just goals and objectives, you'll quickly dive into the nitty-gritty of tasks you want to focus on, people you want to meet, people you want to avoid, conference calls you want to skip, presentations you want to make. And when you think about this strong week and all the specific activities you want to fill it with, you won't recoil from how overwhelming it all is. Instead, you'll feel in control, able to keep it all in your head, able to visualize it. There's just something quintessentially useful about the scale of a week.

And this should be no surprise. A week was designed this

way. It was designed expressly to meet the psychological needs of human beings, something you can't say about any other unit of time. Years, months, and days have nothing to do with us and our needs. They are predetermined by the movement of the earth around the sun, or the moon around the earth. Hours, minutes, and seconds are abstractions created by us to give clocks and watches something to measure.

But weeks are something special. They are not driven by any planet's movement, and they are not an artificial unit of measurement necessitated by some recent piece of machinery. They are ancient—thank the very ancient Sumerians for inventing them. They are virtually universal—the major religions count years from different starting points, break years into varying numbers of months, and designate a different day of the week as the holy day, but they all use seven-day weeks.

And they are highly resistant to modification. The most recent redesign of the week was attempted by the French revolutionaries in 1793, who changed a week from seven to ten days and renamed it, confusingly, a "decade." Needless to say, this redesign didn't last long—more than a "decade," but less than a decade.

All of this is to say that the seven-day week is one of the best weapons you have in your battle to build your entire life around your strengths.

So at the end of each week, or over the weekend, or very early on a Monday, take fifteen minutes to complete a Strong Week Plan. As you'll see from the example below, this plan is wickedly simple. It consists of two dials: one focused backward, where you mark the percentage that you spent playing to your strengths last week, and one forward, where you predict how much of this coming week will call upon your strengths. These are your own assessments, but nonetheless they keep you focused on your trend line: Are your weeks getting stronger or weaker?

The plan then challenges you to identify two specific actions that you will take each week to free your strengths (and two actions to stop your weaknesses, which we'll get to in step four). These two actions will not change your work situation overnight, but as Heidi found, if they are specific enough, and if you discipline yourself to follow through and do them, they will create a ripple effect that, week upon week, will transform how you spend your time at work.

Please go to SimplyStrengths.com each week, print out a Strong Week Plan, and complete it. Then, as the week progresses, try as hard as you can—and as much as your colleagues and boss will allow—to do what you say you are going to do.

Whether or not you use our version of a Strong Week Plan is less important than having one. Take a look at the people in your life who have achieved sustained top performance, and you will see that they have filled their weeks with activities that strengthen them. This didn't happen by accident. Look closer, and you'll see something resembling a Strong Week Plan routine. It might not mirror precisely our version of it, but, nonetheless, each week you'll see them identify one or two activities that, no matter what the week throws at them, they will push hard to do, and one or two activities they will push equally hard to avoid.

To replicate their performance, you must replicate this routine. From this day on, devise a plan each week to push *toward* two specific activities and *away* from two others. Do this each week, every week, year upon year, and the changes you want to make in your life will both work and last.

strongweek PLAN™

DATE: WEEK START   WEEK END

1 LAST WEEK

What % of last week did you spend doing things that you really like to do?

50%
25%
75%
0%
100%

2 THIS WEEK

What % of this week will you spend doing things that you really like to do?

50%
25%
75%
0%
100%

3 FREE STRENGTHS

What actions will you take this week to FREE up your strengths?

•

•

4 STOP WEAKNESSES

What actions will you take this week to STOP your weaknesses from getting in the way?

•

•

FOUR STRATEGIES TO PUT YOUR STRENGTHS TO WORK

It's possible that you are the kind of person who, having written your Strength Statements, knows immediately which two specific actions you can commit to this week. If so, good luck to you.

Most of us will benefit from a little prodding. After studying closely people who have managed to stay on their strengths path, and those who have managed to find their way back after taking a wrong turn, we discovered a clear sequence to this prodding.

The word *FREE* captures this sequence well, with each letter referring to a distinct strategy for putting your strengths to work. Whenever you find yourself struggling to identify what you can do this week to capitalize on your strengths, pick one particular strength and then try one of these four strategies.

In this next section, you'll run through each of the four strategies. Then, to get a sense of them in the real world, you'll see Heidi's first pass at each strategy.

YOUR FREE INTERVIEW™

F is for Focus

Strategy 1: Identify how this strength helps you in your current job.
You saw the data showing that 73 percent of us use at least one of our strengths at least once a week. Sometimes we forget this. So, if you want to have a strong week this next week, begin by taking stock of how you currently use this strength to succeed.

The benefit of doing this is not merely that you will feel a little better about yourself—although this benefit shouldn't be sniffed at, since making a change in your life at work is often a matter of changing your outlook on yourself. The main benefit is that you may well discover that you are currently using this strength far more frequently than you first thought. So take the time to take stock.

Of course, this first strategy may prove to be a grim reality check—you are barely using this strength at all, and you can't recall a single instance when you were recognized for it. Sad to hear, but good to know. The way ahead always starts with a "You Are Here" arrow.

Here are four questions to help you take stock of your strength in action.

(Please log on to SimplyStrengths.com and download the entire FREE interview if you don't want to mark up the book.)

You don't have to go into great detail with each of your answers. Just go deep enough so that you know where, how, and why this strength works for you. To give you a sense of it, Heidi's answers are on page 138.

STRENGTH: ....

FOCUS
Identify how and where this specific strength helps you in your current role.

1. When do you get to use this strength at work?
   In what activities?

2. How often do you get to use this strength?

3. When and how has this strength proved really helpful to you on the job?

4. What feedback, if any, have you received about this strength?

STRENGTH:

I help a hotel manager take a good hotel, or hotel group, and make it #1.

F	**FOCUS** *Heidi*
	Identify how and where this specific strength helps you in your current role.

1. When do you get to use this strength at work? In what activities?

   - *When I teach GM leader class*
   - *Plan and conduct a pre-opening or post opening consultation*

2. How often do you get to use this strength?

   20% of the time.

3. When and how has this strength proved really helpful to you on the job?

   Everyday when I work with GMs and Owners.

4. What feedback, if any, have you received about this strength?

   After about a month of results, I have had GMs and Owners call me back, excited about the positive impact and thanking me for my help.

R is for Release

Strategy 2: Find the missed opportunities in your current role.

It's almost guaranteed that there'll be some missed opportunities. It may well be that nobody is actively preventing you from using this strength. It's more that you are not yet putting yourself in quite the right situations. Perhaps your schedule, for no good reason that you can see, requires you to spend a considerable amount of time not using this strength. Perhaps there are a couple of meetings that you probably don't need to attend. There's a different set of meetings that you should arrange instead. There's a process or protocol that could be tweaked to accommodate your strength.

If any of this is going to happen, you probably need to persuade someone—a colleague or a manager—that the results will make it worthwhile. What measured performance increase could you and they expect to see if the meeting, or the schedule, or the procedure, or the protocol was indeed changed? What's your answer when people want justification?

To generate more ideas for what to do this week, ask yourself these five questions:

STRENGTH: ....

R | **RELEASE**
Find the missed opportunities in your current role.

---

5. What new situations can you put yourself in to use this
strength more?

....
....
....
....

6. Can you change your work schedule (shift) to put yourself in
these situations? Do you need to talk to anyone to make this
happen? Who?

....
....
....

7. What new systems or techniques can you try to accelerate
this strength?

....
....
....

8. How can you measure/track how much you use this strength?

....
....
....

9. Are you struggling with any of your current job responsibilities?
Which ones? How can you use this strength to help you
overcome this?

....
....

STRENGTH:

I help a hotel manager take a good hotel, or hotel group, and make it #1.

R	**RELEASE**
	Find the missed opportunities in your current role.

5. What new situations can you put yourself in to use this strength more?

Take more time to do it.

Working with my Key Accounts to help them go from good to great.

6. Can you change your work schedule (shift) to put yourself in these situations? Do you need to talk to anyone to make this happen? Who?

Yes, I need to allow time to accomplish it.

No.

7. What new systems or techniques can you try to accelerate this strength?

• Have a conference call with ownership group to find out their needs

• make it a priority

8. How can you measure/track how much you use this strength?

Look at TQS, Denials and see if revenue is increasing.

9. Are you struggling with any of your current job responsibilities? Which ones? How can you use this strength to help you overcome this?

Yes, doing too many things that are not valuable — chasing hotels. Do more of this and less of that.

E is for Educate

Strategy 3: Learn new skills and techniques you need to build this strength.

By now you may have identified two specific actions that you can take this week. If so, call a halt to your FREE interview, scribble down the actions on your Strong Week Plan, and head off into your week.

If not, or if you want to push yourself to go deeper, move on to the first *E* of FREE.

This strength of yours comes naturally to you—that's one of the reasons why you picked it—but it will still benefit hugely from focused learning and development. This strength is precisely the area where you will grow the most if you bother to invest it with new skills and techniques. Often we forget this. During a regular workweek, we tend to go to where the pain is, and poor performance is where the pain is. So areas of poor performance get the training; areas of struggle get the shoring up.

We discussed the power of this myth in step one. To neutralize its power in your life, push yourself to identify specific skills that you can learn to sharpen this strength. Volunteer for classes where you are already highly proficient. Seek out people who are even better than you at employing this strength and watch them, take them out to lunch, job shadow.

You might think that others will disapprove of your trying to get better at things you're good at, but the opposite may well turn out to be true. They'll not only appreciate your mastery as you keep sharpening your strength, you'll also earn a reputation as someone who's not satisfied with his current level of performance, which is, of course, never a bad thing to be known for.

Here are four questions to get you thinking about how to sharpen your strength:

STRENGTH: ....

 EDUCATE
Learn new skills and techniques to build this strength.

10. What new skills can you learn to leverage this strength?

....
....
....
....

11. What actions can you take to learn these skills? Are there books
you can read, classes you can take, online research you can do?

....
....
....
....

12. Who can you job shadow at work?

....
....
....
....

13. Who can you talk to about how to use this strength more
effectively? (E.g., a friend, teacher, manager, or mentor.)

....
....
....
....

STRENGTH:

I help a hotel manager take a good hotel, or hotel group, and make it #1.

E	**EDUCATE** Learn new skills and techniques to build this strength.

10. What new skills can you learn to leverage this strength?

Not any I can think of.

11. What actions can you take to learn these skills? Are there books you can read, classes you can take, online research you can do?

Research — See if there are some internal best practices that I can use.

12. Who can you job-shadow at work?

Ask some of our sister brands to see how they approach it.

13. Who can you talk to about how to use this strength more effectively? (E.g., a friend, teacher, manager, or mentor.)

Georgia — my manager.

E is for Expand

Strategy 4: Build your job around this strength.

Finally, consider the idea that you could actively expand your role toward this strength and make it much more central to your job.

For example, how can you use this strength to teach others some of the tips and tricks you have discovered? One of the best ways to make your strengths central to your role is to generate new ideas around it, and then take it upon yourself to share these ideas with your colleagues. You'll have to be a little careful how you do this so that you don't come across like a know-it-all. It may help to phrase it as a question, such as "Would it help if you tried it this way . . . ? " Or, modestly, "I've discovered that what seems to work well for me is . . ." Or maybe save your ideas for more formal settings by volunteering to teach new-employee orientations or prepare training materials. So long as you bear this in mind, you'll be surprised how readily others will appreciate the initiative you've shown and will no doubt expect more of it from you. This is all to the good, since what they'll be asking you to do is call upon your strength even more, which is, after all, the whole point of the exercise.

And if you worry that you are not a great teacher, that you don't frequently come up with new ideas, that you are not a particularly creative person, remember this: The wonderful thing about a strength is that it is you at your most creative and innovative.

Because your mind works faster when you are using your strength, you will forever be coming up with nifty new ways of doing things. And because you have an appetite to practice your strength, you will always and impatiently be testing out these new ideas, seeing what works and what doesn't, tweaking the idea, putting the tweaked idea into practice, and refining it all over again. You won't be doing this because someone is telling you to. You'll do it because you can't help it. So you might as well get credit for it. You might as well be asked to do more of it.

And then, what about just getting so good at employing this strength that you force those around you—your boss, your HR department, your colleagues—to consider the heretofore crazy idea that your job should be changed so that it is built almost entirely around your using this strength? You are going to have to get really good at it and have measurable proof that you are adding significantly to the bottom line before they will even entertain the idea, but at least keep your mind open to it.

First, Break All the Rules discussed the basketball star Dennis Rodman as an example of this. He was so dominating a rebounder on the basketball court that he wasn't expected to do much of anything else. Rodman has long since retired, but I've just watched another specialist, England's soccer star David Beckham, curl a thirty-five-yard shot over a wall of opposing players, on a swooping, dipping line into the bottom right-hand corner of the goal to beat the Ecuador team 1–0. As far as I can tell, he did precious little else while on the field except to score this winning goal. Inevitably England wound up falling to the Portuguese on penalty kicks in the next round of matches, but throughout the World Cup tournament, Beckham proved his worth. He had become so overwhelmingly good at bending long-range free kicks into the net that this one strength defined virtually his entire role.

Perhaps you could do something similar in your role. And lest you think that this sort of rarefied specialization is only for superstar athletes, keep reading. As you'll learn in step five, Heidi's role and those of the rest of her department have recently been expanded to make the strengths of each person central to his job.

STRENGTH: ....

EXPAND
Build your job around this strength.

14. How can you share your best practices around this strength with others? When can you do this?

_____

_____

_____

_____

_____

_____

_____

_____

_____

15. How can you expand your role to make better use of this strength?

_____

_____

_____

_____

_____

_____

_____

_____

STRENGTH:

I help a hotel manager take a good hotel, or hotel group, and make it #1.

E	**EXPAND** Build your job around this strength.

14. How can you share your best practices around this strength with others? When can you do this?

• Get Jeanne involved with this concept.

• Have a meeting with her next week.

• Have her come up with ideas on using strengths.

• Have her come up with ideas on measuring results.

• Figure out a way to stop doing what you loathe.

15. How can you expand your role to make better use of this strength?

• Diminish what I don't like doing.

• Focus on what I love!

On page 151, you'll see all fifteen questions, and at Sim-plyStrengths.com you'll find the same helpful guide that you can print out and laminate.

There are no right answers to these questions, but there *are* answers—there are always answers. You are not entirely at the mercy of your company, your manager, or a rigid job description. You can take many actions to mold this job description so that it calls upon your strengths. So, each week, push yourself to get specific about exactly which actions you will be taking this week. Complete your Strong Week Plan. And if you are stumped for actions to take, go through the FREE interview. There is always a way forward. The right questions will help you find it.

ASK A FRIEND

Sometimes other people can help you find it. We'll get more specific about this in step five, but right now know that you may benefit from having one of your colleagues ask you these FREE questions. You may be one of those people who lets yourself off the hook rather easily and needs a little push from someone else to get you to drill down and search around for truly powerful answers. Or perhaps your personality is like Heidi's, in that you need to involve other people in your life; you thrive under the close scrutiny of people who know you well, challenge you, and expect the best of you. If so, you'll find that the FREE questions work quite well as an actual coaching interview.

Before you go through it with your colleague, however, there are three things you must be sure to tell him:

First, tell him that it's OK for you to say no to some of the questions. The purpose of the FREE questions is to help you identify which actions you can take this coming week. If a certain question doesn't stimulate any ideas, that's fine. Just move on to the next one. (As you will have noticed, Heidi wrote "No" to a couple of the questions in her interview.)

Second, tell him that you want him to push you to come up with *specific* actions. In the spirit of this, he shouldn't let you get away with making vague commitments such as "I'll try to do more of that" or "I must get better at this." Words such as *more, better,* and *harder* should set alarm bells ringing and should prompt him to follow up along the lines of: "Yes, but what specifically are you going to do?"

Finally, tell him to watch the first film of the *Trombone Player Wanted* series. Sometimes people will get the wrong idea about you and your strengths. They'll think you are being a little self-centered and that you are trying to get out of the daily grind that we all need to put up with. The film will help you explain what you are trying to do with your time at work, and why.

Here, as a reminder, are the four strategies to free your strengths. Each week, if you find yourself struggling to identify two actions to take, turn to the questions within each strategy and use them to spur your thinking. You will always find some way to push the world toward your strengths.

For a video challenge from me about Step 3, visit Simply Strengths.com.

FOCUS™

Identify how and where this specific Strength helps
you in your current role.

1. When do you get to use this strength at work? In what activities?
2. How often do you get to use this strength?
3. When and how has this strength proved really helpful to you on the job?
4. What feedback, if any, have you received about this strength?

RELEASE

Find the missed opportunities in your current role.

5. What new situations can you put yourself in to use this strength more?
6. Can you change your work schedule (shift) to put yourself in these situations?
   Do you need to talk to anyone to make this happen? Who?
7. What new systems or techniques can you try to accelerate this strength?
8. How can you measure/track how much you use this strength?
9. Are you struggling with any of your current job responsibilities? Which ones?
   How can you use this strength to help you overcome this?

EDUCATE

Learn new skills and techniques to build this strength.

10. What new skills can you learn to leverage this strength?
11. What actions can you take to learn these skills? Are there books you can
    read, classes you can take, online research you can do?
12. Who can you job shadow at work?
13. Who can you talk to about how to use this strength more effectively?
    (E.g., a friend, teacher, manager, or mentor.)

EXPAND

Build your job around this strength.

14. How can you share your best practices around this strength with others?
    When can you do this?
15. How can you expand your role to make better use of this strength?

STEP 4

STOP YOUR WEAKNESSES

"HOW CAN YOU CUT OUT WHAT WEAKENS YOU?"

WHAT ARE YOUR MOST DOMINANT WEAKNESSES?

Now, what are you going to do with all those red pages, those bitter reminders of the activities in your day that weaken and drain you? It's tempting to want to burn them. Perhaps have a ceremonial cleansing, where you watch the pages shrink in the flames and float away in curls of smoke, a dark offering to the Gods of Wasted Potential.

Unfortunately, physically getting rid of those pages, while temporarily satisfying, won't remove the activities they represent in your day-to-day life. In fact you'll want to keep those pages close to you because stopping your weaknesses is just as important (some would argue even more important) than freeing your strengths. To paraphrase the great military strategist Sun Tzu: Keep your strengths close and your weaknesses closer.

You want to keep them close because what you don't know can hurt you. Like enemies, weaknesses are more dangerous when they are quietly corrupting your work and life. By becoming intimate with the activities that weaken you and labeling them for what they are, you can to take steps to stop their rotten work.

First, you can box them in. You may not be able to dispatch them completely, but by tagging them as activities to avoid, you are better able to contain them within your regular work schedule. Activities that weaken you are like dirty time bombs, waiting to spread their cloud into your strength time—time you could be spending on the activities that make you feel strong. By identifying these toxic activities and naming them, you'll be able to recognize them the moment they appear and either navigate around them or suffer through them for only a finite amount of time. In effect, you can shut them up in a lead box and neutralize them. Itemized, close, safe.

Second, you'll be able to see them in their proper perspective. Most likely you've had some bad weeks at work, weeks that put you in such a foul mood that it seeped into your weekends and personal life. When this happens, it's easy to be seduced by sweeping statements of dissatisfaction:

"It's my boss. She doesn't understand me or the demands of the job."

"My job has changed for the worse and won't ever get any better."

"This company is just crazy."

The bomb has exploded, its cloud has enveloped you, and is now poisoning your entire outlook on life at work.

While it may feel like your entire job is contaminated, that's probably not true. In reality, just a few activities are ruining your days, corrupting everything else in your job. By identifying, naming, and tagging them, you restore them to their actual size: little puffs of annoyance, not a radioactive haze.

The goal of this step is to help you stop these weakening activities from infecting your workweek. Of course, this being a not-quite-perfect world, there will still be some activities that you just can't drop cold. Fine, so it goes. But for those activities that you can't stop doing outright, there are other strategies you can use that will allow you to dramatically cut the time you spend on them.

The positive side of all this is that it will put you in a position to regain control over the toxic activities that fill your day. The flip side, of course, is that once you acknowledge and gain power over these activities, you don't get to whine about them anymore.

CAPTURE, CLARIFY, AND CONFIRM

The Signs of a Weakness

To begin, turn to those red pages. Obviously, I don't know how many pages you filled with "I Loathed It" activities—I've seen as many as twenty-five in a week and as few as four. Regardless of the overall number, what you are looking for are the three activities whose influence on your time at work you would *most* like to lessen. Flip through the pages and consider what you wrote. Try to put yourself back at the very moment when the prospect of the activity or actually doing the activity prompted you to scribble something down. Try to zero in on those three activities that generated strongly negative emotions and are regular parts of each week.

To help you, look for the clearest signs of a weakness, which are, as you would expect, the inverse of the strength signs. These signs will prove useful not just in pinpointing your three most dominant weaknesses but also in spotting future potential weaknesses before they spread and contaminate your entire work.

S is for Success (or rather, the lack of it)

Which of your red pages involved activities where the outcomes weren't at the level you were hoping to achieve? Look closely at the activity and ask yourself if you have repeatedly tried this type of activity before and not enjoyed any real success with it. Perhaps people—friends, bosses, family—have mentioned that you need to improve in this type of activity, or perhaps you yourself have sought out some remedial training. Now ask yourself if you have ever been praised or received prizes or awards for doing this type of activity. Don't go easy on yourself. Your own unblemished truth about where you have repeatedly struggled to succeed is your first and most obvious sign of a weakness. So take off those rose-tinted spectacles and start here.

However, as with your strengths, your weaknesses encompass more than merely activities you are bad at. In fact, as the reluctant swimmer Matt Borden discovered, you may actually be rather good at them. Remember, the most useful definition of a weakness is an activity that makes you feel weak. It's an activity that, no matter how proficient you may (or may not) be at it, consistently produces negative emotional reactions.

To give you a sense of the emotions at play here and what is ultimately at stake, look at those red pages again. Read each one closely, and as you read, pay attention to what your body is doing. Do you feel your shoulders begin to hunch, your back begin to tighten ever so slightly? Has your brow started to furrow, even imperceptibly? And how is your breathing? The same as before you started reading or perhaps just a little faster, a touch shallower? Seeing the activities that you've written in your own hand brings you right back to how you were feeling when you were doing that activity, and it's surprising how quickly those bad feelings express themselves in your physiology.

And how about your handwriting? Looking at it now on the red pages, you can probably tell that the lines are written a little harder. The penmanship is most likely rushed and slightly less legible. A little amateur handwriting analysis, and you can decipher anger and frustration. The words may even be trailing down instead of rising up, the classic handwriting "tell" for pessimism.

There's passion here, strong emotion. What's good about this is that, as with your strengths, you are the leading authority on your own emotions. You look at these red pages and you know better than anyone else exactly what you were feeling when you were doing the activity. If you are quite proficient at a couple of them, over the years other people might have tried to persuade you that you like doing them, or even that you *should* like doing them. But you know how you really feel. You are the true expert on what weakens you.

So take your time and look for the other telling signs of a weakness.

I is for lack of Instinct

Your weaknesses have a "no matter how hard I try, I just can't get excited by the prospect of this" quality to them. In many ways, a weakness is akin to an allergy to nuts or shellfish or bees. You may not have the words to explain why these things repulse you or scare you or hurt you, but you know from prior experience that they always do and always will. No matter how hard you try to like them, the outcome will always be the same: negative.

When you're confronted with a weakening activity, you first look for ways to avoid doing it. Next you think there must be someone else who can do this activity instead of you. Then finally, after going through the denial phase (where you just don't want to do it) and the hope phase (someone will rescue you from the task) comes a bracing acceptance, where you eventually hold your nose and try to do what's required. Avoidance, searching for someone else to do it, and having to brace yourself: all good clues that you lack the instinct for it.

G is for lack of Growth

And then, when you are doing it, all you can think about is when you can stop. You aren't inquisitive about it. You don't want to get better at it. You don't want to read up on it and learn more about it. It's just barren and boring, so much so that when you are doing it, you struggle to concentrate. Your mind starts to wander, and you find yourself hoping for an email or a phone call—or an earthquake—anything to distract you, anything but having to keep doing the activity.

Sure, you may experience this inability to concentrate even when you are not involved in a weakness—when you are tired, perhaps, or when you are just about to gear up for a high-pressure situation. But some activities *consistently* create in you symptoms very similar to adult attention deficit disorder. You may have developed coping mechanisms to get through these times, but as soon as you release your focus, your mind drifts, and you find yourself looking up at the clock, which, strangely, seems not to have moved at all. It's the "clock of the long now." You're living in weakness time, a time where the present moment is horribly stretched, and bad feelings seem to last forever.

N is for lack of Needs

And then finally it's over. The activity is done.

But, perversely, the bad feelings are not. They linger. You sit there and ask yourself yet again, "Why do I have to put myself through this?" You feel not only physically tired but also emotionally and intellectually drained. Unlike the activities that strengthen you—which, as you would predict, fill you up with feelings of satisfaction and power—activities that weaken you seem to defy physics. They manage to fill an emptiness with a greater feeling of void. And this void is not neutral. It feels like loss, like the opposite of winning.

This is one of the reasons why it's so important to take steps to cut out your weaknesses. The time right after you're done with one isn't back-to-normal time. Instead, right afterward, you feel less like yourself, less optimistic, less creative, less resilient, less productive, and less willing to saddle up again and take on the world. You're still in weakness time.

In your mind's eye, you cringe when you think back on yourself doing this activity. There's not even a hint of the equation where time plus distance gives this activity a sweet tinge of nostalgia. It was a drag after you did it. It's a drag when you think about it now. The only thing that makes you happy thinking about this activity is contemplating a world where you would never have to do it again.

Flip through your red pages and pay attention to these four signs. If you find that you never volunteer for a certain activity, take the hint. If you find that you don't look forward to a certain activity, take the hint. If, when you're doing an activity, you struggle to concentrate, and time slows to a crawl, take the hint. If never having to do an activity again would still be too soon, take the hint. These are weaknesses. They weaken you. There may be no good reason why, but they do. So identify them and own up to them. If you don't, like enemies, they will derail your best-laid plans.

Quit "Should-ing"

At this point, a word of warning is necessary. When you're looking over your red pages and searching for your three most dominant weaknesses, there is one thing you need to be vigilantly aware of, something that may well prevent you from accurately picking out what weakens you: should-ing.

For example, say that one of your red pages reads:

"I loathed being responsible for John's work. He may be my direct report, but he never gets it right!"

Should-ing can be heard in that faint but unmistakable voice in your head saying, "At this stage in my career, I *should* want to be responsible for other people's work."

Or say that you've written "I hated having to make that presentation to my sales team," and the should-ing voice says, "If I want to get promoted, I really *should* be making regular presentations to my team."

All down the line, you can more than likely look at any of those statements you've written and think, "Well, I really *should* be more organized," or "I *should* want to make cold calls to develop new customers," or "I *should* take on writing the group's strategic plan for next year."

This voice is powerful and persuasive, but you must not listen to it. If those activities make you feel drained, frustrated, or burned out, you *should not* be doing them, or at least not much of them and not for long.

Should-ing is a by-product of our cultural obsession with being well rounded and the prevailing corporate demand that we capitalize on our so-called areas of opportunity. If you've accurately captured the activities that weaken you, the chances are high that you are never going to love doing them. When told you have to make a presentation to your team, your first thought is "Do I have to?" As for designing a system to organize your work flow, your eyes glaze over just reading the words *work flow.*

Don't feel bad about this. Accept it. Trying to conjure up a yearning for a task just because your boss or society or even you yourself think it's something that you *should* do is a recipe for both disappointment and poor performance.

Probably the best example of a person who rarely listens to this should-ing voice is Warren Buffett. He may have billions more dollars than you and me, but nonetheless he is subject, as we all are, to powerful social pressures and expectations. One of them, albeit unwritten, states: After acquiring your massive fortune, you should be actively interested in philanthropy. In the face of this, his decision to donate the vast majority of his personal wealth ($31 billion) to the Bill and Melinda Gates Foundation confounded a great number of people. Why would anyone with that much money—and wisdom and talent and Nebraska goodness—be willing to allow someone else to manage, and in the long run take the credit for, the distribution of his philanthropic donation?

When asked why he was giving his money to the Gateses, Buffett had a twofold answer. First, and most predictably, he said, "They can give it away better than I can."

We would expect this kind of no-frills pragmatism from Buffett. He has never been tempted by the dramatic, attention-getting gesture. Instead, he has always focused on what is most effective, on what exactly will get the job done. His gift to the Gates Foundation can certainly be understood in these terms.

But then he followed up with this much more surprising statement:

"Besides, philanthropy isn't fun for me. Running my businesses day-to-day is fun for me. Philanthropy just isn't something I enjoy thinking about every day."

Can you imagine the amount of self-possession it takes to confess that it bores you to think about philanthropy? No one, no matter how wealthy, is supposed to be bored by philanthropy. We might each have our own cause célèbre—you may be passionate about improving literacy, while I am ardently up in arms about poverty—but regardless, we *should* all have a cause.

Buffett confessed that he didn't have a particular cause. He came clean to the world and said he's much more intrigued helping Borsheims—one of his companies—drive up its margin on its engagement rings than he is by driving up child inoculation rates. The challenge of helping Nebraska Furniture Mart—another Berkshire Hathaway company—sell another sofa invigorates him viscerally in a way that slowing the spread of AIDS never could.

This confession revealed a remarkable strength of character. Despite society's expectations of him, Buffett remained clearheaded and strong willed enough to say, in effect, "Philanthropy weakens me, and it always will, so I am choosing to hand it off to someone who is strengthened by it."

This didn't mean that he dismissed or disrespected philanthropy. In fact it meant the opposite. By making his donation, he was saying: "I admire the goals of philanthropy. In fact I admire them so much that I cannot allow them to be undertaken by a guy like me."

If you are to identify accurately your weaknesses, you must be similarly clearheaded and strong willed. No matter what others may tell you, when you confess that a certain activity weakens you, this does not mean that you disrespect the activity any more than Warren Buffet disrespects philanthropy. It simply means that this activity consistently creates in you negative emotional reactions. In which case, as Buffet did, the most respectful, responsible, and lastingly effective thing you can do is figure out a way to cut it out of your life.

Clarify

Before we get into the practical matter of how to do that, take a moment to clarify the three activities you picked from your stack of red pages. As you did with your strengths, use those "Does it matter . . . ?" questions to create three Weakness Statements that are specific enough to capture the intensity of your feelings but generic enough to guide you into next week and beyond.

To recap, these are the four questions:

1. Does it matter *why* you are doing it?
2. Does it matter *who* you are doing it with/to/for?
3. Does it matter *when* you do it?
4. Does it matter *what* it's about?

Sometimes these questions will yield little new information; what you wrote on the red page perfectly and completely captures the activity that weakens you. Change the tense from the past ("I loathed it when . . .") to the present ("I feel weak when . . ."), and you have your Weakness Statement.

For example, one of the activities that made it to the top of my red stack was:

"I loathed it when I had to attend a cocktail-party reception after my presentation to XXX company."

I am often invited to these sorts of events. Either pre- or post-presentation, I will be asked to do a meet and greet with a select group of people. On the surface, these events aren't terribly demanding. As the people mill around in their small clusters, all I have to do is move from one cluster to another, introduce myself, nod, smile, tell a couple of my stories, listen to a couple of theirs, and then leave.

But for some reason I dread them. Tell me that I have to jump up onstage and talk to a thousand people, and I'll actively look forward to it. But ask me to come work a room right before or right after, and my hackles go up. I pace my hotel room, hoping for a call that the event is cancelled, and if not, try to time my arrival so that I am not so late as to be rude, while still managing to leave as few minutes as possible for the actual mingling.

It's not that I don't know how to mingle, and it's not that I'm terrible at it. It's just that I never look forward to it, and I'm exhausted afterward. Two sure signs of a weakness.

After running this activity through the "Does it matter . . . ?" questions, this is what I got:

Q. Does it matter why I am doing this activity?
A. No. Any mingling drains me. Mingling to make friends drains me just as much as mingling to make business contacts does.

Q. Does it matter who I do this activity with/to/for?
A. No. A cocktail party after my sister's wedding, with all my closest friends and relatives? Bad. A fifth birthday party for Jackson, with all his little friends and their parents? Bad. A meet and greet with a high-powered group after sharing a platform with General Colin Powell and President Bill Clinton? Still bad.

Q. Does it matter when I do this activity?
A. No. Right after a speech or right before, early in the morning with coffee or during cocktail hour, when I've something important to do right afterward or when I'm in the midst of a vacation, all bad.

Q. Does it matter what this activity is about?
A. No. And I suppose that's part of the problem for me. Mingling with a group of forty to fifty people is never about anything. In fact, the essence of it is that you are supposed to be able to flit graciously from one conversation about nothing to another conversation about nothing. Why would you ever want

to put yourself in this situation, a situation where you will be forced to have a series of meaningless exchanges, asking questions you know will lead nowhere, nodding when the other person nods, catching his eye as he scans the room over your shoulder, or feeling guilty as he catches you doing the same, always searching for that one perfect question/answer combination to provide you with the polite exit so that you can finally move on and have yet another meaningless exchange? I mean, really, what a complete waste of time!

This isn't the point I was initially trying to make, but did you see what I just did with my answer to the last question? I did what so many of us do with our weaknesses. By choosing to describe it in a rather extreme way (though in truth I found myself writing the paragraph above, rather than actively choosing to write it this way), I transformed my weakness from an activity that happens, for no good reason, to weaken me, into an activity that is universally wrong, morally wrong. "I mean, really, what a complete waste of time!" I turned something that I *happen* to feel into something that everyone *should* feel.

Social scientists label this the "naturalistic fallacy," the confusion of *is* with *ought,* as in "because men tend to be more aggressive than women, men *ought* to be more aggressive than women."

Weakness spinning is a better term. Keep alert for it. Listen closely, and you'll be able to catch yourself (and others) weakness spinning like crazy. It's tempting because it turns what is a personality quirk into something much more socially acceptable, namely, a commonly held "bad thing." Nonetheless, you must avoid weakness spinning as much as you can because it stops you from seeing a personal quirk for what it is: a personal quirk. And therefore it stops you from dealing with it properly.

My original point was simply that none of the "Does it matter . . . ?" questions altered the activity I had scribbled down on my red page. Thus, after asking each of them, I wound up with this Weakness Statement:

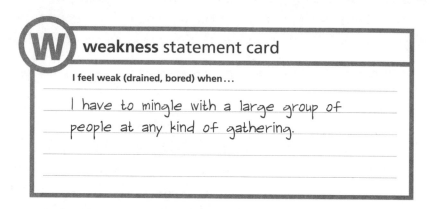

weakness statement card

I feel weak (drained, bored) when...

I have to mingle with a large group of people at any kind of gathering.

You may discover something different, though. By asking the "Does it matter . . . ?" questions, you may reveal to yourself the one key element about the activity that makes you feel so weak.

For example, you may discover that it's not that you hate emails. You just hate being copied on emails that have nothing to do with your work.

You don't hate participating in all meetings. You hate two-hour meetings scheduled at 9:00 a.m. on a Friday.

You don't dislike new projects. You dislike starting new projects that last longer than four months.

You don't feel weak when you are responsible for other people's work. You feel weak when you are responsible for the work of novice people who you are now supposed to train.

As with your strengths, it's the specifics of a particular activity that are most revealing and the most actionable. So take the time to subject each of your three red pages to those questions. Be patient. Look closely for the critical details and then write three Weakness Statements that are vivid, specific, and that capture the essence of what bugged you enough to write them down in the first place.

And, as before, if you experience no emotion when you re-read them, you aren't there yet. Emotion generated these statements, so you should feel emotion when you read them. If you don't, go back to the red page, ask yourself the four "Does it matter . . . ?" questions, and try again.

Confirm

Finally, you'll want to confirm that these three are indeed your most dominant weaknesses. To help you, on the next page you'll find a Weakness Test (also available at SimplyStrengths.com):

If an activity scores 53 or above, this is a true weakness; your version of Kryptonite. You must immediately take steps to cut this activity back to a bare minimum or deliberately skew your time away from. Avoid it at all costs. It will make you look weak and ineffective.

If it scores 46 to 52, it is less a weakness and more of a weak spot. It won't completely undermine you, it will just diminish your capacity. Done occasionally, with people you like and really want to help, and preferably right after you've used one of your strengths, you can handle it. But put you under pressure, with people you don't like much and whose intentions are unclear, and right after doing another weakening activity, and you will crack. Under these conditions, this weak spot will be exposed and will likely hurt you and your reputation. So stay especially vigilant for when exactly you are undertaking this activity, and try as hard as you can to do it only when you are at your strongest.

If it scores 37 to 45, it is not really a weakness, it's a potential pitfall. It doesn't happen that often, and when it does, on most days, under most conditions, you can handle it. At worst, it

Weakness Test™

Look for **SIGNs** of a weakness

On a scale of 1–5, 1 = *strongly disagree* and 5 = *strongly agree*, write down your responses to the following statements:

S = Lack of SUCCESS

1. I have tried this type of activity repeatedly with little success.   1 2 3 4 5

2. Other people often tell me that I need to improve in this type of activity.   1 2 3 4 5

3. I have received no prizes or recognition for doing this type of activity.   1 2 3 4 5

I = Lack of INSTINCT

4. I look for ways to avoid doing this type of activity.   1 2 3 4 5

5. I keep thinking of other people who can do this type of activity instead of me.   1 2 3 4 5

6. I have to brace myself to do this type of activity.   1 2 3 4 5

G = Lack of GROWTH

7. I took a long time to learn this type of activity.   1 2 3 4 5

8. This type of activity bores me.   1 2 3 4 5

9. No matter how much I try, my performance in this type of activity doesn't get much better.   1 2 3 4 5

N = Lack of NEEDS

10. This type of activity leaves me feeling tired and drained.   1 2 3 4 5

11. I cringe when I think back on myself doing this type of activity.   1 2 3 4 5

12. It makes me happy to think of a world where I would never have to do this type of activity again.   1 2 3 4 5 could trip you up. So when you can, step around it. And when you can't avoid it, be bold enough to ask for people's patience and understanding. Ask them to tread lightly with you. (More on how to do this in the next step.)

If the activity scores less than 37, it's really not worth bothering about. I suppose you could take steps to minimize it, but, frankly, this time would be far better spent figuring out how to free one of your strengths. If your most draining weakness scores less than 37, the best advice is to thank your lucky stars and then do everything in your power to maximize your strengths.

Now that you've captured, clarified, and confirmed three Weakness Statements, I strongly recommend that you do what you did with your Strength Statements and find a way to preserve and highlight them. Write them in the cards below or log onto SimplyStrengths.com and complete the Weakness Statement cards you'll find there. You can then either print them out or save them electronically.

As you did with your strengths, you need to learn your Weakness Statements by heart. Your weaknesses will not often present themselves to you as weaknesses, the equivalent of a round, black, cartoonish bomb with a long fuse hissing and crackling, waiting to explode. Instead they tend to be hidden behind something much more appealing, like, say, a promotion, or an opportunity to volunteer for a high-profile project team, or a favor to a colleague—or, as Warren Buffett discovered, as a noble role that everyone expects you to play.

Your three Weakness Statements will keep you alert for the hidden bomb. Once you've seen it for what it is, there are still many courses of action open to you. You may refuse it, or defuse it, or accept it and then figure out how to protect yourself from it—but at least you'll be making an informed choice. At least you'll be in control.

W weakness statement card

I feel weak (drained, bored) when...

_____
_____
_____
_____
_____

W weakness statement card

I feel weak (drained, bored) when...

_____
_____
_____
_____
_____

W weakness statement card

I feel weak (drained, bored) when...

_____
_____
_____
_____
_____

BACK TO YOUR STRONG WEEK PLAN

There's a natural thought that comes to mind when we spend focused time detailing all the weakening activities in our job. It sounds something like this: I've got to get out of this job!

That's normal. But it's also the most radical thought you should entertain. You have to trust the fact that if you follow this six-step discipline, changes will happen. They will take time and effort and maybe even a little mental manipulation on your part, but if you discipline yourself to hone in on the activities that weaken you, you'll be amazed—no matter how regimented or bureaucratic your organization—at how pliable your job description really is.

Now, if you're thinking that you want to be a physicist, and you're currently working as a chef, sorry, no amount of incremental change in your current job is going to help you achieve your goal. And of course we can't rule out the notion that your appetites and your current position have evolved to the point where they are entirely out of sync. It is certainly possible that the weakening activities filling your days and weeks have achieved a critical, soul-destroying mass, and so moving on to a different role is the best solution.

And it's also possible that your organization or company has recently made major changes to your job description to further its ends, and that these changes have dragged you away from those activities that invigorate you. In which case, again, a move may be required.

However, before you make this final decision, give your current role a chance. It may be that the perfect role for you is hiding in plain sight, beneath layer upon layer of the wrong activities. With a little discipline, you may be able to peel away these activities, and, week by week, reveal a role that plays to your strengths.

To get started, complete another Strong Week Plan, but this week, rather than identifying two actions to free a strength, pick two things that you can do this week to stop one of your weaknesses. If you want to use the plan on the next page, go ahead.

strongweek PLAN™

DATE: WEEK START   WEEK END

1 LAST WEEK

What % of last week did you spend doing things that you really like to do?

50 %
25 %   75 %
0 %   100 %

2 THIS WEEK

What % of this week will you spend doing things that you really like to do?

50 %
25 %   75 %
0 %   100 %

3 FREE STRENGTHS

What actions will you take this week to FREE up your strengths?

•

•

4 STOP WEAKNESSES

What actions will you take this week to STOP your weaknesses from getting in the way?

•

•

Or, if you want to leave the book unmarked, log onto Simply Strengths.com and print out one from there.

FOUR STRATEGIES TO STOP YOUR WEAKNESSES

You may be one of those lucky people who know immediately what two actions they can take. If so, write them into your Strong Week Plan and then set about your week.

But if you aren't so lucky, here are four strategies to help you figure out how to minimize the amount of time your weaknesses take or the amount of distress they cause. As you did with your strengths, first select from your top three weaknesses the one that is currently proving most damaging to you. More than likely, it will be the one that scored the highest when you ran it through the Weakness Test.

Then, once you've selected it, consider each of these four strategies:

1. Stop doing the activity and see if anyone notices or cares.
2. Team up with someone who is strengthened by the very activity that weakens you.
3. Offer up one of your strengths, and gradually steer your job toward this strength and away from the weakness.
4. Perceive your weakness from a different perspective.

A little later in the step, you'll learn more about each of these strategies and use the STOP interview to discover which of them best applies to the weakness you've selected. However, for the moment, turn your attention back to Heidi. These four strategies were derived from a study of people who were extremely effective at keeping their weaknesses under control. Most of these people found that one or another of the four strategies worked best for them. As you'll see, Heidi found a way to apply them all. I'm not suggesting that you will or should. Nonetheless, study what she did. Her experience will show you what happens when these four strategies meet the real world.

HEIDI STOPS CALLING

After completing the capture, clarify, and confirm process on her large stack of red cards, Heidi wound up with these three Weakness Statements:

W | **weakness** statement card

I feel weak (drained, bored) when...

I have to chase hotels to turn in, or respond to, something that is much too late.

W | **weakness** statement card

I feel weak (drained, bored) when...

I am reading unimportant emails.

W weakness statement card

I feel weak (drained, bored) when...

I am dealing with negative people, including those who don't want to improve or make changes.

Nothing too dramatic here, except for the rather obvious fact that her current role required her to do each one of these every day. So, to begin the discipline of pushing her time away from these weaknesses, she selected the one that took the greatest toll on her energy and resilience—the first one—and then made a series of small adjustments until she had shrunk it down to a manageable size and stripped it of its most negative aspects.

This is what Heidi did:

First, she decided to stop calling her most disengaged hotels. She didn't stop for one week or even for one month. She decided to stop calling them for an entire quarter. Today she isn't too proud to admit that the idea of just dropping these hotels from her call sheets scared her. This wasn't some nice-to-do activity; it was deeply lodged into her daily routine, a core component of her job description as a brand director. How could she just stop chasing these hotels? What would her colleagues say? Would her boss freak out when she told her? And what would happen to the hotels? Would they become an embarrassment to the Hampton family?

Scary though these questions were, the fear of repercussions from dropping her problem hotels was nothing compared to the sense of dread she felt each time she got ready to go to work. So she plowed ahead with her plan for a quarter of abstinence. For Heidi, no measure was too drastic if it meant finding a way to stay engaged, stay productive, and stay with Hampton.

And what were the repercussions? Nothing. Her colleagues didn't notice. Neither did her boss. And the hotels? At the end of the quarter, Heidi went back to her analysis reports and scrolled down to see what impact her benign neglect had on the hotels. To her surprise: not much. "Those hotels just stayed exactly where they were," says Heidi. "Even after ignoring them for three months, they didn't drop any further. They basically performed the same whether I called or I didn't."

Of course Heidi realized that not every problem hotel could just be ignored. Some merely needed more leveraged incentives. For example, if she found herself calling a hotel manager to remind him of a corporate promotion and wasn't getting a response, instead of fretting and repeatedly calling the scofflaw manager, Heidi did something different. "I went straight to the franchise owner and politely let him know the situation and how not implementing the program was going to negatively impact his bottom line," she says with a laugh. "I may not have control over those managers, but the franchise owners do. And let me tell you, nine out of ten of those repeat offenders whose bosses I called delivered on what I was asking them to do."

Heidi was lucky in the sense that there were a number of people on her team going through the strengths program (including her boss), and they were starting to have conversations about where each was strong and where each was weak. "It made it easier to take some risks," Heidi says. It also made Heidi realize that she had colleagues who actually loved to do what she loathed and vice versa.

Over the course of her career, Heidi, like many of us, had teamed up with other people to swap certain tasks in which she found no joy. "When I was a general manager, I didn't like doing sales," remembers Heidi. "I still don't like making cold calls and finding new accounts, yet as a GM I was responsible for sales." So Heidi asked her assistant manager, who was into making sales calls, if he was willing to take on those duties in exchange for something else. "He just loved making relationships and closing deals. In exchange, I did all the paperwork that he loathed doing. My boss didn't know how the sales were getting done, but they were getting done, and everyone was happy."

Now, armed with her new strengths-based perspective, she could transform this from a catch-as-catch-can make-do into a deliberate performance strategy. This proved useful a couple of months later when Heidi was suddenly presented with a project that looked like it would force her back into the role of chasing hotels. Hampton was planning its annual summit conference, a critical event that provided Hampton corporate with an opportunity to communicate key initiatives for the coming year to all the franchisees. Unfortunately, getting all the franchisees and GMs to sign up was as frustrating as cat wrangling.

Heidi's boss, Georgia, knew it was going to be difficult, so she offered each brand director $300 in discretionary funds that they could use as an incentive. Heidi racked her brain to figure out how to manage around having to call up and chase all those hotels. Her first idea fizzled. She offered one hundred of her most challenging hotel managers a chance to win $100 if they filled out the necessary forms by a certain deadline. When the date arrived, only fifteen of the hotels had responded. So much for a cash incentive.

Now truly desperate not to fall back into old habits at the first hurdle, Heidi remembered the deal she'd made with her cold-call-loving assistant manager. If she could find just the right person this time, maybe it would work again. So she looked around the office, ran each person through her mental check list of his or her strengths and weaknesses, and landed on a colleague, Shelli. Shelli's job had nothing to do with getting hotel GMs to sign up for the yearly summit, but over the years Heidi had noticed that Shelli loved the phone. At the slightest provocation she would pick it up, make the call, and soon be chatting up just about anybody.

Heidi approached her and offered her this simple deal: Heidi would pay Shelli $50 if she could get a certain percentage of the remaining hotels signed up, and an additional $100 if she could get them all. "Shelli not only gets a kick out of the phone, she also just loves a challenge," says Heidi.

Shelli immediately agreed. Besides the money, Shelli saw it as a chance to play to her own strengths. "I knew Heidi hated the idea of having to call all those hotels, but I just love doing that, getting to know people and starting to build a relationship with them," says Shelli. "For me the project was an opportunity to connect with all those GMs out there before we met them face to face at the summit."

When Heidi shared with some of her other colleagues what she had done, she was surprised by their reactions. "Some people in our department got mad and thought it was unfair," says Heidi. "I just reminded them that Georgia said we could use the three hundred dollars however we wanted. I don't think she expected me to use the money the way I did, but it fit in with our whole strengths-based approach, and it helped get the job done. So why not?"

In the buildup to the summit, Shelli managed to get all but ten of the hotels signed up. By then, Heidi's take on the task had changed. Her competitive nature was sparked. "At that point, it started to feel almost like fun. Getting that last ten made me want to win," says Heidi. Invigorated by looking at the task from this different perspective, Heidi jumped on the phone, called the remaining ten, signed them up, and completed the project with a 100 percent sign-up rate. Give credit where credit is due: Shelli received the full $150 bonus. (And Heidi returned the remaining $150 to Georgia, unspent.)

"It made me realize how you can not only use someone else's strengths to accomplish a goal, but also that this is how all of Hampton should be building our teams."

Heidi wasn't alone in that line of thinking. After her manager, Georgia, witnessed Heidi's success with the strengths program (as well her own and the other participants'), she decided to reorganize the whole department around each person's individual strengths.

We'll learn more about how this was done in the next step, but for now, you should know that Heidi's role has changed completely. She had been made responsible for training and supporting new hotels that are just joining the Hampton family. "My days at work are so different now," she says. "I don't call up the challenging hotels and try to muscle them into doing something they don't want to do anyway. Instead I get to work with enthusiastic new GMs who really want to learn, who are hungry for best practices, and eager to get their hotel up to speed as quickly as possible. They all want their hotel to be number one, but they know they don't have all the answers. They realize they need to keep their eyes and ears open for the programs and tactics that really work. Every week I get a new audience of people who are primed to push me to give them better and better ideas. I just love it."

And who's chasing now? As one part of the brand team's realignment, Georgia created a new position that is dedicated to chasing those hotels that struggle. Only now, the interview process and selection of candidates for the role is based on finding people who are strengthened by the very activities that so weakened Heidi.

YOUR STOP INTERVIEW

Heidi came up with her actions by herself, as you will need to. But she was prompted to do so by the STOP interview. This interview takes you through each of the four strategies and challenges you to find a way to take action this week.

To identify the most effective actions for you, choose one weakness and run it through the interview. As with the FREE interview, you can either answer these questions by yourself, or involve a colleague or trusted friend.

S is for Stop

Strategy 1: Stop doing the activity and see if anyone notices or cares.
This seems like a recipe for getting yourself fired, but there are many occasions where it proves surprisingly effective. Before you try something more complicated, at least consider the possibility that you could just stop doing it.

As you saw, this was Heidi's first move. And the strange thing was, despite the fact that chasing lagging hotels was supposedly a cornerstone of her job, when she stopped doing it, no one even noticed. You may well find the same.

Organizations tend to be outstanding at starting new projects, procedures, activities, and work streams, and terrible at stopping them. Some crisis or emergency will demand a response, or some new executive will arrive with her pet approach, and so the organization will launch a new initiative. Roles will be changed, performance requirements altered. Then inevitably the crisis will pass, the executive will move on, but the new initiative and its accompanying activities will linger on, like satellites shot into space, never to come down, hanging over your head, once vital, now useless. Space waste.

Take a long, hard look at the weakening activity. It may well be space waste.

Consider these four questions:

WEAKNESS: _____

S	**STOP** Doing this activity.

1. Is this activity/weakness critical to your success on your job? If yes, go to question 3.

_____

_____

_____

_____

2. Is there a way that you could just stop doing it? If yes, go to question 4.

_____

_____

_____

_____

3. If you can't stop doing the activity, how can you reduce the amount of time you spend on it?

_____

_____

_____

_____

4. Who would you need to talk to, if anyone, to make this happen?

_____

_____

_____

WEAKNESS:

I have to chase hotels to turn in, or respond to, something that is much too late.

S	**STOP** Doing this activity.

1. Is this activity/weakness critical to your success on your job? If yes, go to question 3.

Only partially — my results from chasing are not good. I am not really making a huge impact.

2. Is there a way that you could just stop doing it? If yes, go to question 4.

Yes, to some extent.

3. If you can't stop doing the activity, how can you reduce the amount of time you spend on it?

I can be selective on who I chase — those that I think I can impact.

4. Who would you need to talk to, if anyone, to make this happen?

nobody — I am just going to do it and see what happens. Will anyone notice??

I will need to get Jeanne's buy-in also.

T is for Team

Strategy 2: Team up with someone who is strengthened by the very activity that weakens you.

You now know that your pattern of loves and loathes will more than likely not match up perfectly with your job description. Many activities will invigorate you, but, unless you are exceptionally lucky, many others will bore you, frustrate you, or deplete you.

The good news is that your colleagues will not share your distinct pattern of loves and loathes. Now, it's possible you are so close to your own strengths and weaknesses that you can't quite imagine that there could be someone else out there who actually loves what you loathe. For example, since you loathe filling out your expense reports, you can't conceive that someone could actually look forward to doing them—you might be able to imagine someone being more willing than you are to put up with doing them, and you can certainly pick out people who are far better than you at doing them, but finding someone who loves doing expenses? No, never.

But of course there is someone out there like that. In fact, although you wouldn't know it from looking at her, Heidi loves doing expense reports. "There's nothing quite like getting all the receipts organized and making it all balance," she says, grinning. "During my worst weeks, I would save up my expenses and do all of them at the end of the week just to perk myself back up and raise my spirits."

I'm not suggesting that you necessarily get someone else to do your expense reports—many companies require you to do them yourself. What I am suggesting is simply that you look around you. Maybe you work with someone like Heidi, someone who loves to do something that, in your mind's eye, no one

WEAKNESS: ....

T | **TEAM UP**
With others who are strengthened by this activity.

5. Who do you work with that really likes to do this activity?

6. How can you arrange to swap activities? (E.g., you do what he/she doesn't like and vice versa.)

7. Who could teach you a trick or technique for how to do this activity more quickly/efficiently?

8. How can you make this activity more fun to do? (E.g., is there somebody you can do this activity with, or can you make a game out of this activity?)

WEAKNESS:

I have to chase hotels to turn in, or respond to, something that is much too late.

T TEAM UP
With others who are strengthened by this activity.

5. Who do you work with that really likes to do this activity?

Not that I know of, but will research. I will ask Jeanne.

6. How can you arrange to swap activities? (E.g., you do what he/she doesn't like and vice versa.)

Jeanne does not like to chase either — so not for now.

7. Who could teach you a trick or technique for how to do this activity more quickly/efficiently?

Will research —

8. How can you make this activity more fun to do? (E.g., is there somebody you can do this activity with, or can you make a game out of this activity?)

Yes, Jeanne and I can partner on the hotels that will give us the greatest results. At the end we can measure who was more successful.

could possibly love. If you can find that person and negotiate some kind of trade, you will achieve a powerful win-win.

O is for Offer Up

Strategy 3: Offer up one of your strengths, and gradually steer your job toward this strength and away from the weakness.
Time and resources are finite. Hence, no matter how they are spent to begin with, organizations will gradually spend most time and resources on those activities that add the greatest value, and less on those that add comparatively less value.

This is good news for you. It means that if you can repeatedly push yourself into situations that play to your strengths, your organization will, over time, see the value it is getting, and will gradually devote more time and resources to these activities. The company won't do this because it will make you happier but because it's getting better performance outcomes.

Of course a welcome by-product is that less and less time will be available for those weakening activities. If you keep pushing to play to your strengths, if you keep volunteering, and keep showing the value of what you do, your role's entire focus will shift until finally there's no time left at all for those weakening activities.

This is what Heidi did. She kept showing Georgia the financial payoff from taking good hotels and making them great. In the end, virtually all of her time and resources became focused on this. Perhaps you could do the same:

WEAKNESS: ....

O | **OFFER UP**
A strength and steer your job toward it.

9. Which of your strengths can you use to get this activity done more easily?

10. How can you gradually carve a new role for yourself by regularly volunteering your strengths?

WEAKNESS:

I have to chase hotels to turn in, or respond to, something that is much too late.

OFFER UP

A strength and steer your job toward it.

9. Which of your strengths can you use to get this activity done more easily?

I can use my analytical strength to look at my list of hotels and determine where my greatest impact would be and focus my efforts there.

I can also review my current approach and determine if there is a better way to get results.

10. How can you gradually carve a new role for yourself by regularly volunteering your strengths?

Start looking at where I can make a larger contribution. Focus on those areas and cut back on doing things I dislike.

P is for Perspective

Strategy 4: Perceive your weakness from a different perspective.

Inevitably, there will be some activities that you can't stop doing, that don't match up with someone else's strengths, and that you can't navigate away from. Faced with this type of activity, don't resign yourself to just suffering through it quite yet. Try this last strategy. See if you can change your perspective on the activity so that it doesn't prove quite so draining.

Of course the most effective perspective will be a strengths perspective. Look at the activity through the lens of one of your strengths, and you might well be able to transform its effect on you.

Sometimes this will be as simple as changing the time of day when you do the weakening activity. For example, whenever I have to confront someone—something I loathe—I wait until the end of the day, after I have got some strength-based activities under my belt and am feeling strong and invigorated. I use my strengths to overpower my weakness. Don't take my approach as gospel, however. Heidi did the exact opposite. Whenever she had to call a particularly challenging hotel, she would do it first thing in the morning. She always felt stronger in the morning, and by doing it then and getting it out of the way, it didn't build up in her mind and contaminate the rest of her day. The bottom line: Figure out what's right for you.

Sometimes it will require more mental gymnastics from you than simply changing the time of day. You will have to discipline yourself to see the activity in the service of one of your strengths rather than just hanging out there all by itself as a weakness. For example, if you loathe planning meetings but love serving guests, shift your perspective to see how this meeting will result in better guest service. If you loathe confronting people but love the feeling of follow-through, shift your perspective so that you see the confrontation as merely one step in following the project all the way through to completion. If you loathe doing budgets but love being viewed as a vital member of the team, shift your perspective to see how doing the budget will ultimately help the team.

You may never turn the weakness into a strength, but, as Heidi discovered when it got down to the last ten hotels to sign up, and she started to view the activity through the lens of her competitiveness, you may actually find yourself looking forward to it.

WEAKNESS: ....

P | **PERCEIVE**
Your weakness from a different perspective.

11. How can you shift your perspective on the way you do the activity?

....

....

....

12. Would it be helpful to do this activity at a different time of day?

....

....

13. How can you look at this activity through the lens of one of your strengths?

....

....

....

14. How will doing this activity support you in maximizing your strengths? (E.g., organizing my desk so I can find customer files more quickly.)

....

....

....

15. What connection, if any, can you make between this activity and something that interests you or is really important to you?

....

....

....

WEAKNESS:

I have to chase hotels to turn in, or respond to, something that is much too late.

P PERCEIVE
Your weakness from a different perspective.

11. How can you shift your perspective on the way you do the activity?

Look at this as an opportunity to train new General Managers. On the non-responsive hotels skip the GM and go to the owner.

12. Would it be helpful to do this activity at a different time of day?

Yes — move it to the morning so I can get it over with!

13. How can you look at this activity through the lens of one of your strengths?

Look at it as a training opportunity. Can I inspire and engage them to turn in their work?

14. How will doing this activity support you in maximizing your strengths? (E.g., organizing my desk so I can find customer files more quickly.)

If I can drive quick results I can spend more time with GM's maximizing revenue.

15. What connection, if any, can you make between this activity and something that interests you or is really important to you?

Nothing I can think of ... Would like to eliminate chasing if possible.

Here as a reminder are all four strategies and the accompanying questions. When you find yourself struggling to identify what you can do to stop one of your weaknesses, turn to these four strategies, ask yourself the questions, and take action. You will always have more room to maneuver than you think.

For a video challenge from me about Step 4, visit Simply Strengths.com.

STOP™
Doing this activity.

1. Is this activity/weakness critical to your success on your job? If yes, go to question 3.
2. Is there a way that you can just stop doing it? If yes, go to question 4.
3. If you can't stop doing the activity, how can you reduce the amount of time you spend on it?
4. Who would you need to talk to, if anyone, to make this happen?

TEAM UP
With others who are strengthened by this activity.

5. Who do you work with that really likes to do this activity?
6. Can you swap activities? (E.g., you do what he/she doesn't like and vice versa.)
7. Who could teach you a trick or technique for how to do this activity more quickly/efficiently?
8. How can you make this activity more fun to do? (E.g., is there somebody you can do this activity with, or can you make a game out of this activity?)

OFFER UP
A strength and steer your job toward it.

9. Which of your strengths can you use to get this activity done more easily?
10. How can you gradually carve a new role for yourself by regularly volunteering your strengths?

PERCEIVE
Your weakness from a different perspective.

11. How can you shift your perspective on the way you do the activity?
12. Would it be helpful to do this activity at a different time of day?
13. How can you look at this activity through the lens of one of your strengths?
14. How will doing this activity support you in maximizing your strengths? (E.g., organizing my desk so I can find customer files more quickly.)
15. What connection, if any, can you make between this activity and something that interests you or is really important to you?

STEP 5

SPEAK UP

"HOW CAN YOU CREATE STRONG TEAMS?"

Up until now you've been working on your strengths and weaknesses largely on your own. You've been paying close attention to the activities that make up your days and weeks at work, and you've written down how each of those activities makes you feel. And, assuming you did the work of crafting your three Strength and Weakness Statements, during the last two steps you've hopefully figured out how to steer your time toward your strengths and away from your weaknesses.

Granted, the work you've done thus far has by no means been easy. On the surface, it might sound simple to say, "I want to spend more time on activities that strengthen me and less time on activities that weaken me." (I can't begin to count the number of times people have responded to that statement with "Who doesn't?") But as you've no doubt experienced, there's a chasm between saying and doing, a chasm that takes focus, self-discipline, and not a little faith to cross.

Now, in step five, you're going to do something that is as tricky as anything you've done so far and will require even more faith. You're going to speak up and get help. Specifically, you're going to go up to your manager and have a strong conversation with him. You're going to describe to this person what strengthens you and what weakens you, and you're going to have to do it in such a way that he winds up thinking not that you're trying to make life easy for yourself but, rather, that you are a responsible colleague looking for ways to contribute more—and at the same time make *his* life a little easier. By the time you're done, he must not only understand you better, he must actively want to help you maximize your strengths.

Pulling off a conversation like this in the real world of work is admittedly a bit daunting. As we described back in the introduction, much more common are conversations where workers and their colleagues or managers tiptoe carefully around one another, giving away just enough to advance their interests, and little more. Somehow, in those situations where it matters the most for us to reveal ourselves, we struggle the most to express ourselves.

To reach outstanding levels of performance, you must stop tiptoeing. You must learn how to express—using unambiguous words and examples—what strengthens you and what weakens you. If you don't know how to have these conversations, there'll always be a limit to how much you'll be able to redirect your time at work toward your strengths and away from your weaknesses. You'll push and push, but, lacking other people's understanding and support, you'll keep bumping up against the rigid walls of your job description, their job descriptions, and your manager's boxes on his organizational chart.

At first glance, it seems like it might actually be quite easy to have these conversations. Why wouldn't other people want to learn about your strengths and weaknesses? After all, they should want you to use your strengths, not only because you will contribute more but because they in turn will get to use their strengths more, and so contribute more, and be more productive, and happier, and more creative.

Yet spend even a little time imagining one of these conversations, and you'll see why, despite serving everyone's interests, they often get stymied. To give your imagination some grist, meet Christine and her manager, Martin.

"YOUR STRENGTHS WEAKEN ME"

Christine (a pseudonym) is director of program development at a training company in Southern California catering to Fortune 500 clients such as Coca-Cola, Yahoo, Toyota, and Best Buy. Her job is to design the training programs, and then, once they have been sold into a company, to deliver them.

Like each of us, Christine has a number of distinct strengths. One of them is that she is invigorated by training trainers to be better. She loves nearly every aspect of the teaching process. She loves seeing the satisfaction the trainer feels when his students excel and the growth in his own confidence as he becomes more comfortable with his material. She has a third eye for fine distinctions, for the subtleties in how a trainer presents information and why those nuances make a big difference in turning students' confusion into understanding. So there's little that Christine looks forward to more than getting on the phone with one of her trainers and pinpointing these nuances. She'll offer to sit in on his sessions, and at the end, provide surgically precise notes on where the session went perfectly and why—and how, with a couple of tweaks—the students' learning could be deepened or accelerated.

Interestingly, she's not particularly adept at doing what she's training her trainers to do. She's not great at standing up in front of a classroom full of corporate students and owning the room with her presence and the power of her delivery. Sit her down in a room with five senior trainers who want to dive into the details of program design, and she excels. But increase those numbers to twenty-five, turn the trainers into students, and tell Christine to hold their attention for a full day's training, and she's mediocre.

She's not invariably a great teacher, yet she's a great teacher of teachers. It may seem a bit strange, but most of us, when you look closely, have a combination of strengths and weaknesses that is not entirely predictable.

Strange or not, the challenge for Christine and her manager, whom we'll call Martin, is to figure out how to exploit this distinct strength for the benefit of her company and its clients. They have a lot to talk about. Together they have to figure out how to design a train-the-trainer product based on her strengths, how to market it, price it, and select a specific group of clients on which to focus it. They have to decide what kinds of materials are necessary and whether Christine is the right person to create them. They have to decide the optimal number of trainers Christine is capable of working with and how frequently she should check back in with them to assess their competence.

These are the kind of details that will determine just how productive Christine's strengths are at work. Given how critical her performance is to the entire company, she and Martin should be talking about them virtually all the time.

Unfortunately, this is not what they are talking about. Most of the time, Christine and Martin talk about "clarity reports"; specifically, how Christine can get better at doing them.

Why are they discussing this? Because Martin likes clarity reports. He has a million things going on in his world at any one time, and he wants it this way. For him, working with multiple projects that spin into other projects, and making sure that each one is progressing in parallel is what makes life interesting. To help him manage so many projects, he's devised this thing called a clarity report.

It's a spreadsheet that captures every aspect of Martin's world at work, and it's really quite impressive. To some it would seem as confusing as the chalkboard of theorems and formulas in a particle-physics classroom, but to Martin it's a thing of beauty. It's a living representation of all the different tasks and clients and obligations he's currently working on. It's got columns going out to double alphabetical reference points and rows linked to different worksheets where every cell details an activity, a timeline, a progress status, and a reference number. He just loves it. Walk by his office, and he's sitting there, staring at it, smiling. Ask him about it, and he'll admit to waking up in the middle of the night with thoughts about how to make his clarity reports even more clarifying. While it might seem to some that Martin is a bit, shall we say, obsessed, his clarity reports strengthen him. And, of course, they help him get the work done.

And since Christine works for Martin, she is supposed to fill out her own clarity reports and submit them to Martin so that he can be aware of what she's up to.

This, to put it mildly, weakens her. Ask her how she defines her approach to work, and she gives a clear though diametrically opposite answer to Martin's: "I think strategically," she says, "and execute randomly." Christine doesn't find any clarity in Martin's invention. In fact, when she tries to do them, she feels thoroughly confused. As a result, she doesn't do them very well. Talk to Christine about clarity reports, and the calm authority she exudes when instructing her trainers lurches into staccato sentences that seem to career off a cliff and shatter on the rocks beneath.

She knows it too. When she first saw one, she felt a gut reaction, a prick of panic in her throat. And now when she gamely tries to complete one, her mind becomes blank, dull, and time moves very slowly. She puts it aside for a while, hoping for a stray feeling of enthusiasm, which never comes, and the waiting begins to look a lot like procrastination, which it is. The procrastination makes her feel bad, so she tries to knuckle down and do it, but the darn thing shuts down her mind again, and now she starts to panic, and there it still is, sitting on her desk.

These are some pretty strong reactions—reactions that most certainly distract her from putting her strengths to work—so you'd think that she would immediately make Martin aware of them. Does she? Well, no, not really. Yes, she has mentioned once or twice that clarity reports "aren't easy" for her, but she has never actively pushed back and said, "Sorry, Martin, your clarity reports weaken me. I don't want to do them anymore." Of course, she hasn't said that. No one who wants to keep her job says that.

Instead she turns in on herself. Christine is a good team member, a responsible trooper who wants to do the right thing. Besides, she really likes Martin, so she says to herself, "Well, OK, all right, maybe I need to try a little harder and really apply myself to it. If I'm going to make Martin happy, I should do it. And if I'm going to get a promotion, I should do it. And if I want the biggest bonus possible at year's end, I really should do it."

On a rational level she knows better than this, but caught in the busyness of day-to-day working life, she allows herself to be swayed by the unspoken logic of life at work: Do what your boss wants, and your life at work will go smoothly.

The specifics of Christine's and Martin's situation might be new to you, but it's a sure bet that their dynamic is familiar. At some point in your career you will have found yourself hemmed in by a manager who prides himself on a system that doesn't fit you; a manager whose very strengths weaken you. And although this situation usually causes you to become intensely frustrated with your manager, it's not really his fault. Yes, in a perfect world Martin should realize that his system doesn't apply to everyone, but in the real world Martin simply wants to get a bunch of stuff done. Viewed through his lens, the only way to do this successfully is by organizing and arranging and prioritizing and moving things forward in parallel paths in perfect sequence. In other words, a clarity report. He doesn't take this view because he wants to impose his rigid bosslike ways on his employee. He takes it because, like the rest of us, he relies on his strengths to get the job done. And doesn't he have a right to use his strengths just as much as Christine does?

Of course he does.

Tragedy, so it's said, is not the battle of right against wrong, it's the inevitable clash of right against right. In this sense, Christine's and Martin's failure to communicate is almost tragic—or at least a sad comedy of errors. Christine capitulates to what she thinks Martin wants from her, and Martin keeps asking Christine to do what he would do if he were in her situation. Does that make Martin a bad manager? Does it make Christine a weak employee? Not really. It's just another unfortunate but commonplace misstep of the working world, the outcome of which, as with all such situations, is waste: Martin and Christine are not talking in detail about how to put Christine's strengths to work, and, as a result, they are wasting many opportunities for Christine to do something spectacularly valuable for their clients. Which is, ironically, what they both want.

Common though this situation is, it doesn't have to be this way. To all the Christines out there, it might feel as though there's no exit, but look closer, and you'll see that there is a way out. Furthermore, Christine, not Martin, holds the key.

It's not Christine's fault that she succumbed to the status quo of office politics—it happens to the best of us—but when it comes down to it, she's the one who can fix her situation. She's the one who knows her strengths and weaknesses better than anyone, so she's the one who has to *push* her world, which includes Martin, toward her strengths and away from those things that weaken her. It's tempting to expect Martin to take the lead because we've come to believe that it's our manager's job to tell us what to do and how to do it. But for the most part, that's just not true.

And until you realize that it's not your manager who controls how you spend your days and weeks at work, that it's not your manager who decides what your strengths and weaknesses are, that it's not your manager who controls which activities you spend more time on and which activities you spend less time on, you will continue to be a victim of someone else's circumstances. And you will never perform like you should.

But as you will see, there are ways to break out. Christine can have the right conversations with Martin and her colleagues so that they learn where they can expect the most from her, and she from them. Then everyone, beginning with Christine, can be challenged to put his or her strengths to work for the benefit of the team.

As you read on, and as you decide whether to pause and actually have the conversations we suggest, remember: The person who benefits from these strong conversations is not only Martin. It's also Christine. There are many reasons why the world hasn't yet lined up around her particular strengths and weaknesses, but the biggest one is that she hasn't yet spoken up and told the world clearly enough what they are.

SO WHAT ARE YOU AFRAID OF?

By now Christine knows vividly what her strengths are, as vividly as you know yours, and so, pumped up with this self-knowledge, it would be tempting for Christine to waltz right into Martin's office and confront him with her truth: "I am invigorated by training trainers and weakened by clarity reports."

But she is too savvy for that. She knows that, taken by surprise, Martin's first reaction would be suspicion that Christine is trying to get out of doing something. Your manager may have the same reaction. Not necessarily because he is a congenitally suspicious person, though he may be, but because it's frightening for a manager to be confronted by an employee who says that his way of doing things drains her or frustrates her. Your manager is held accountable for your performance, which is inherently frightening, and the way he alleviates this fear is to exert some form of control over what you do, normally by telling you how you should do your work. If you walk in and tell him that his "how" weakens you, then you are going to run smack into his fear of losing control. He understands his "how"; he gets it instinctively. Whereas your "how" is alien, unknowable, and therefore scary to him.

You can't dismiss this fear as bad management. It's not. It's a natural reaction to the fact that someone who works for him, someone whose performance he is responsible for, wants to do things in a way that he doesn't intuitively understand.

And while we're on the subject of fear, before you charge off to confront your manager, you should face up to your own fears. Not that they will ever go away completely, but by identifying what they are, you reduce the likelihood that they will trip you up at the critical moment. For example, when it comes time to share your strengths with your manager, you may fear that he will think one or more of the following:

"She is bragging."

"She thinks she's better than anyone else on the team."

"She wants to do only those few things at work that invigorate her."

"She is not a team player."

"She is concentrating more on what makes her happy than on what actually needs to get done around here."

"If these are her strengths, then maybe they're not compatible with the role she's in; maybe I should move her to another role."

Similarly, when you talk with him about your weaknesses, you may fear he'll think:

"She's not competent and can't do her job properly."

"She's lazy and just doesn't want to do the work to get better at her weaknesses."

"She's just difficult. Too much trouble. Why do I need to listen to her, when I could just seek out a more well-rounded team player who doesn't hassle me so much?"

Not all of these fears will ring true for you—you may be a preternaturally self-assured person or be blessed with a deeply empathic manager—but most of them will. Not because you are a fearful person but because you live in the real world. You have seen people have conversations with their managers that didn't go well. You've seen how companies try to control employees through long lists of competencies and accompanying performance appraisals. You've seen how quickly employees can be discarded if they earn a reputation as difficult. Because of all you've seen, your fears, whatever they may be, are legitimate.

To help you through these fears, follow this sequence of conversations. Of course, you'll want to vary the exact content of each one according to your unique situation, but if you ignore the sequence, or skip parts of it, your chances of getting other people to want to help you will fall sharply.

CONVERSATION 1: THE STRENGTHS CHAT

Start by having a chat. Not a "goal-setting session" or a "performance review" or anything like that. Just a chat with someone you're close to about what you've discovered about your strengths over the last five weeks. This person could be a family member, a friend, a work colleague, or even, in rare instances, a boss. But no matter who this person is, her defining characteristic is that she cares about you and wants you to succeed.

During this chat, you are not trying to persuade her of anything, or gain her approval, or even ask for her help. You are simply asking that she listen to you, that she be your audience as you try to find the best way to describe your strengths.

You need this chat because the chances are you are still not very good at talking about your strengths and weaknesses. Listen to people talking at work, listen closely, and you'll soon pick up that conversations at work are hyper-rational. You'll hear discussions about goals, targets, processes, process improvements, budgets, analyses, strategies, market shares, units, and growth curves. This hyper-rationality applies not just to the business itself but also to the people in the business, where you'll hear terms like *abilities, skill sets, experience levels, leadership style, selling style, promotability*, and *high potential*.

We're all comfortable with this language. We're familiar with its grammar, slang, and hidden meanings. It feels like the right language to use at work, a world governed by the twin dispassionate gods Profit and Loss. And in many ways it is.

But it's the wrong language to describe strengths and weaknesses. As you know, the language of strengths and weaknesses is a fundamentally emotional one. To capture your strengths properly, you will have to use phrases like:

"This thrills me."

"I love this."

"I can't wait to . . ."

"I get so excited by . . ."

And to do your weaknesses justice, you'll have to resort to similarly emotional phrases:

"I can't stand it when . . ."

"I feel wasted when . . ."

"I'm so bored by . . ."

You know how to use this language to describe other aspects of your life—your relationships, your hobbies, your family—but not your work. Emotions, with the possible exception of competitiveness, are largely out of place at work. In a world ruled by the need to analyze and compromise and fit in, emotions are entirely too categorical, too powerful, and therefore too difficult to flatten out and control. To gain the support of your boss and your colleagues at work, you are going to have to learn how to wield this emotional language in such a way that you communicate the truth about your strengths and weaknesses but don't leave them petrified that you're a geyser of emotion ready to explode at any moment.

How can you learn this? You practice. First you practice with the easier of the two, your strengths. You call your close friend and you ask her for a chat, which you set up by telling her something along the following lines:

"Look, I've been doing this program for the last few weeks, and the idea is that I need to get better control of my strengths and weaknesses so that I can contribute more. Could you chat with me for a half hour and just listen to me describe what three of my strengths are? And with all due respect, please bear in mind that I'm not interested in whether you agree with me or not, but rather in whether you understand what I'm describing. So the only thing I'm asking you to do is tell me if you get confused. OK?"

Once she's said yes, which surely she will—you chose her precisely because she is the kind of friend who says yes to requests such as this—follow this flow:

- Read your first Strength Statement.
- Give her two vivid examples of when you used this strength in the last week.
- Explain precisely how this strength helps you in your job.
- Do the same with your other two Strength Statements.
- Then, of course, thank your friend and end the chat.

The entire chat will probably take about thirty minutes, perhaps a little more if she asks a lot of questions. Which she may do. And questions are good. They'll push you to seek better words to capture your strengths, more vivid examples, clearer connections between your strengths and what you are actually paid to do—all of which will prove invaluable when your manager, not your best friend, is asking the questions.

When this chat is over, and you feel this close friend has

listened, and heard, and understood, set up another chat with another close friend. Yes, this feels repetitious, but I urge you to do it anyway. You'll need the practice. How else will you find the phrases that work for you, the word combinations that sound like you but are not clichés? Even more important, how else will you try out your examples and push yourself to become even more specific and vivid?

Even though these chats are with your close friends, you need to enter into them as seriously as you would a conversation with your boss. If you don't practice with your friends, then undoubtedly your manager won't understand you, and it won't be your manager's fault.

Then your job won't change in quite the way you want it to, and it still won't be your manager's fault.

CONVERSATION 2: "HOW I CAN HELP YOU"

So now you're ready to talk with your manager about what you would actually like to do differently, given what you've discovered lately about your strengths and weaknesses.

The best advice: set up a "How I can help you" meeting. The point of this meeting is for you to describe to your boss just one of your strengths and exactly how you can exploit this strength to advance a specific project or improve a certain performance outcome. You don't want to have a conversation with her where you describe each of your strengths and weaknesses; it's the rare boss who either would have the time for this kind of navel gazing or would be able to understand and appreciate the subtle distinctions of each of your strengths and weaknesses when spelled out one by one.

What you want to do is collaborate with her, which means that you want to figure out how one of your strengths can help you and her *get something done* together. So pick one strength, and pick one performance outcome that could be affected by this strength, and go into the meeting prepared to lay out precisely how this particular strength can drive this particular outcome.

No matter how much your manager may like you, what she likes even more is getting things done. She likes initiative, so be armed with practical ideas about exactly what you want to do differently, and how, and when, and by how much. Put some numbers to the changes you want to make, and a timeline, and, as much as you can, avoid words such as *more* and *better*. She likes focus too, so make sure the outcome you want to drive fits with the team's overall goals. If it's something you've all been struggling with lately, so much the better.

Here is what you should do before the meeting:

- Call to schedule time with your manager. Make sure that you are both able to focus. Don't do it on the fly or in a group meeting. You want to create an environment where you can have your manager's full attention.
- Let your manager know why you want to speak with her. Give her the background information she needs and explain the outcome for the meeting. It's important that you frame this conversation in such a way that your manager wants to have it and sees the value in having it. For example, you might say:

"Hi, _____. I was wondering if I could schedule half an hour with you some time next week. As you might know, I've been going through this program and have been learning a lot about how I can get my job done even more efficiently. I'm really committed to supporting the team in the best way possible and would love to

share with you some of my ideas about how I can contribute more. I've got a couple of specific things I think would really help us."

And here's a plan for what you should say during the meeting:

"Hi, _____. Thanks for taking the time to meet with me today. As I shared with you when I set up this meeting, I want to talk about how I can make a greater contribution to the team. One of the things I've been doing these last few weeks is identifying all the activities that invigorate me, and that are important to my job, and trying to figure out how I can do more of them in my current role. The idea is that if I can increase the amount of time I spend on activities I'm passionate about, the more productive I'll be. So here's what I am thinking: I know that one of our goals as a team/ one of the projects we are working on is _____

[insert description of project and project outcomes] _____

_____

_____

"One of my strengths is _____

[insert description of strength] _____

_____

_____

_____

"And here's how I think we could leverage it/it would be useful:

_____

_____

_____

_____

"What are your thoughts?" _____

_____

_____

_____

_____

Agreed actions/timelines: _____

[insert actions that you and your boss agree would help this project]

_____

_____

_____

Stick to this flow as closely as you can. Your manager may well interrupt you, so be ready with a quick "parry" phrase to keep the meeting on track, such as "I understand that we still need to address XYZ issue, but please just bear with me for a moment." Even if your boss's questions distract you from the flow, your overall goal is to come across as a volunteer. You want your boss to leave this "How I can help" meeting thinking three things, in descending order of importance:

1. "He's got great ideas for how to help the team. I never would have thought of them."
2. "He's got far more initiative than I realized."
3. "He knows himself really well."

If you can achieve this, you will have set yourself up perfectly for the subsequent conversations you are about to have: namely, those dealing with your weaknesses and how she can help you minimize their impact.

Just to be clear, you did not start with your strengths so that you could soften her up to be more willing to help you with your weaknesses. The whole point of this strengths-based approach to work is to figure out how you can contribute more, and volunteer more, so it just makes sense that your first substantive meeting with your boss should focus on strengths.

However, as a side benefit, this first meeting will now serve as the context for any subsequent meetings you have. The fact that you were so positive in it, so focused on what you wanted to do to be even more productive, will undoubtedly help.

CONVERSATION 3: THE WEAKNESS CHAT

Let a couple of weeks go by—you've been living with your weaknesses for a while, you can live with them for a couple of weeks longer. Then call one of those close friends of yours who knows you well, cares about you, and genuinely wants the best for you, and set up another chat. This time, tell her you want to chat about some of the things that weaken you. But as before, you don't really want her advice. You just want her to listen, and, if she ever becomes confused about what you're describing, suggest that she ask you to clarify.

This weakness chat is critical—even more important than the strengths chat—because during it you must practice two skills that you're not yet very good at but must master before your next meeting with your manager.

First, you must get good at claiming a weakness as a weakness, rather than pawning it off as something else. Look at your three Weakness Statements and try saying one of them out loud. Seriously, try it.

What phrase did you use? Did you just read what was on the card? "I feel weak when . . ."

Or did you say "I feel bored when . . ."? Or "I feel frustrated when . . ."?

Or did those phrases seem false, prompting you to resort to some other phrase, such as "I'm just not comfortable when . . ." or "I get annoyed when . . ."?

No matter what phrase you picked, you'll notice that it probably didn't sound very strong when you said it. Try another phrase.

It still doesn't sound very strong, does it? You can keep trying if you want, but what you'll discover is that no phrase to describe one of your weaknesses sounds anything other than weak.

And since weakness is not normally the impression you want to leave at work, your tendency will be to try to tweak the phrase so that it sounds more positive and assured. So, for example, you might find yourself saying "I feel challenged when . . ." or "I'm not quite at my best when . . ."

Try to avoid this. Try not to give your weaknesses a positive spin. As hard as it may be initially, just read what you wrote on the weakness card. You've identified some activities as weaknesses because they consistently create in you bad feelings, feelings that deplete you, lessen you. There's no point, now that you actually want someone to help you navigate away from these activities, to hide them under positive-sounding words and phrases. So, during your weakness chat with your friend, you need to claim them. Own up to them clearly and precisely. Practice saying your Weakness Statements out loud, using the phrase you wrote on the card. Hear yourself actually saying it and then feel what it's like to let the sentence hang there, out in the open, unqualified.

It won't be a good feeling, and it won't be familiar. The urge to qualify it in some way, to excuse yourself in some way, will be nearly overpowering. Resist it. You need to master claiming your weaknesses because, if for no other reason, you are going to have to do it in front of your manager.

Having said this, I nevertheless suggest two phrases that, out of all of them, seem to be most socially acceptable.

Either: *"It just seems to take me a really long time/I'm really inefficient when . . ."* Claiming inefficiency somehow feels less damning than claiming weakness.

Or: *"I just don't seem to have many good ideas when . . ."* No one is creative and innovative in every aspect of his work, so to admit that a certain activity makes your mind work more slowly may well prove easier for you.

The second skill you need to learn is the art of the comeback. You need to master this because, in conversation with either your close friend or your boss, you won't be the only one feeling funny about leaving your Weakness Statements hanging there between the two of you like dirty laundry. Have you ever noticed that whenever you confess to somebody, whether at home or work, that you struggle with something, or don't like doing something, the other person can't leave it alone? They can't just let it be a thing to be understood about you and worked around in some way. Instead their knee-jerk reaction is to tell you what you should do to get through it. Thus, if Christine were to confess to a friend, a colleague, or even to Martin that she struggles with clarity reports, they'd most likely offer up a "practical" tip such as:

"Oh, it's not that hard if you write it out on paper before you enter it into Excel."

Or they'd try to jolly her along with:

"Oh, it's not that bad once you get into it; you'll see."

Or they'd challenge her with some piece of worldly wisdom:

"Well, we all have some things we don't like doing at work. Stick at it, and you might find that having some bad stuff at work makes you appreciate the good stuff even more."

This advice is all very well intended, of course. But it's not what you want. You don't want to learn some trick to get better at this weakness, and it won't become easier once you "get into it," and you don't need this weakness so that you can fully appreciate your strengths. You just want to figure out how to navigate around it so that it doesn't drag you down as much as it does now.

To ensure that the conversation stays on track, you must learn how to deflect this well-meaning advice. Some version of this phrase works best:

"Thanks. But what I noticed is that no matter how often I do it, it always seems to slow me down. What I really want to do is spend less time on it so that I can do more and achieve more with my strengths."

That last line is the critical one. No one can argue with that, especially with "achieve more." So, during your weakness chat, make sure that you use some version of it a few times. Get your mouth around it and hear yourself saying it. It will undoubtedly prove helpful when talking with your manager.

With all this in mind, I suggest that your weakness chat should flow as follows:

- Read your first Weakness Statement.
- Give her two vivid examples of when this weakness has slowed you down.
- Do the same with your other two Weakness Statements.
- Thank your friend and end the chat.

Later in the same week, call another friend and do it again.

CONVERSATION 4: "HOW YOU CAN HELP ME"

Now you're ready for the next meeting with your manager. This time it is less "How I can help you" and more "How you can help me." The point of this meeting is not the same as your weakness chat. You are not going to list each of your weaknesses and describe examples of how they undermine you. Very few managers could stomach a meeting like that.

And you want her to stomach it. This might sound odd, but, ideally, you want her to actually look forward to it. Here is how you can pull this off.

First, the point of the meeting should be to ask your manager to help you figure out how to be more productive. It's not to complain about some aspect of your job or to alert her to some quirk of your personality. You may have to reveal some of your quirks during the meeting, but that's not the point. To reiterate, you are asking for help so that you can be more productive.

To that end, schedule the meeting with your version of this phrase:

"I've done some more thinking since the last time we met, and I've had a couple of ideas about how I can use more of my strengths and get more done. I could use your help, though, so could I get on your schedule for thirty minutes some time next week?"

Then, before the meeting, pick the weakness that distracts you the most from playing to your strengths and develop three or four ideas for how to minimize it. If you find yourself short on ideas, take out the STOP interview and run the weakness through the questions.

As you're doing this, try not to get discouraged if you look at the S and the T of STOP and realize that you can't just stop doing the activity, and you don't have anyone on the team to whom you could hand it off. Keep your mind open to the many other possible strategies out there, particularly those to be found in the P of STOP. Take Christine as an example. She can't just stop doing the clarity reports, and she can neither find nor hire someone to do them for her. Those aren't her only options, though. She could suggest to Martin that she send him a voice mail at the end of the day. Or she could write him an email detailing the status of each of her many projects. Her problem isn't with having lots going on—she likes this. Her problem is looking at these many projects from the perspective of an Excel spreadsheet. If she could change her perspective, she could reduce how much it weakens her.

As it turned out, this wasn't the strategy that she and Martin landed on, but they certainly could have. To be fully prepared for this meeting, you should be armed with a list of possible strategies, any one of which could free you up to exploit your strengths more effectively.

When you think you're ready, follow a similar sequence as you did with the "How I can help you" meeting. Here's essentially what you should say during the meeting, of course adapting the following passage to your own natural way of speaking:

"Hi, _____. Thanks for taking the time to meet with me today. As I shared with you when I set up this meeting, I want to talk about how I can make a greater contribution to the team. One of the things I've noticed is that no matter how often I do it, doing _____ [insert description of weakness] _____ always seems to slow me down. In this sense, I think it's one of my weaknesses. What I really want to do is figure out how to spend less time on it or

manage around it in some way so that I can do more of what we talked about a couple of weeks ago.

"Here are a couple of ideas I had: _____

[insert description of practical ideas] _____

_____

_____

_____

_____

"What do you think? Do you have any ideas for how I can get you/the team what you need in a slightly different way? _____

_____

_____

_____

_____

Agreed actions/timelines:

[insert actions that you and your boss agree would help streamline your contribution]

_____

_____

_____

_____

_____

By sticking closely to this structure and this flow, Christine and Martin found their solution to the "tragedy" of clarity reports. They thought about hiring someone to act as an intermediary, a project manager through whom all project information would flow, but in the end decided the department couldn't afford it. They considered Christine's ideas of a weekly voice mail or email, and even tried it out for a couple of weeks, but Martin found that he was so used to the layout of the clarity report that without it, he couldn't keep all the details organized in his head. He felt out of control. So here's where they ended up: Each week Christine and Martin meet. Christine runs through her project list, and Martin enters it into his clarity report. One hour later, they're done. Christine's happy. Martin feels in control. Both are in sync.

Stopping activities that weaken you isn't rocket science. And the strategies you end up with may not be earth-shatteringly creative. What's important is the discipline: learning how to describe your weaknesses, devising a few of your own ideas for how to manage around them, and, finally, handling the conversation with your manager so that you come across as a volunteer trying to do the most with what you have (which you are), and not a whiner petulantly expecting the world to conform to your desires, which you're not.

TIPS FOR STRENGTHS-BASED MANAGERS

What is Martin's role in these meetings? Well, simply put, it is the role of all good managers: namely, to do everything in his power to turn Christine's unique combination of strengths and weaknesses into real-world performance.

Accurate though this is, it is a little theoretical. If you are one of the Martins of the world, here are a couple of tips that will help you play this role as effectively as possible:

- **Your chief role is to listen to what your employee is saying, affirm what you hear her say, and offer ideas for actions that can be taken.**
  Your role is not to confirm or deny whether or not the employee is right about her strengths and weaknesses. You may be a more objective judge than she is of her performance—though this is debatable. But what is certain is that she knows what strengthens her and what weakens her far better than you do. So listen carefully and believe what she says.

- **What if you can't let an employee stop doing a particular activity?**
  If you really can't approve an employee's request because you absolutely need her to do that activity, fine. There are times when you just have to say, "Look, I need you to do this right now." However, keep in mind that if the activity is something that weakens her, it is not and never will be productive

to ask her to do it repeatedly. After telling your employee that she has to suck it up for now, make it clear that you're open to discussing ways to steer her away from the activity, while still making sure it gets done somehow. It would be a very mediocre manager who tells an employee to suck it up in the present without any future plan to gradually move her away from the weakness and toward her strengths.

- **What if an employee wants to do more of an activity that you know she's really bad at?**

  First, make sure you've accurately assessed the situation by asking yourself the following questions: (1) Have you seen her do this activity regularly enough to support your conclusion? (2) Is it an activity that she has done repeatedly and really isn't good at? (3) Is this an activity that she hasn't had the opportunity to do often, and, perhaps with some guidance, could become really good at?

  It very well may be that you are correct: This person is not strong in this particular area. As the manager, you then need to draw the line and tell her that although her appetite for the activity is strong, her performance is not. Give her an explanation, using focused examples of times when she's tried the activity with no success. Word to the wise, however: People are good at, or will practice to become good at, things they are repeatedly drawn back to. So be completely sure of your assessment before shutting someone down.

- **What if an employee wants to stop doing a lot of activities, and you think it's because he's trying to get out of doing his job?**

  This is possible, of course. If you can back up your assessment that your employee is just being lazy, you might need to move him out of his current role or off the team. But before taking drastic measures, try offering some extra guidance. Ask your employee, "If you were to stop doing this activity that weakens you, how would you spend the extra time? What would you do instead?" Put him on the spot and make him identify how he can replace the weakening activities with ones that strengthen him.

- **What if the job has certain responsibilities that just aren't going to change? (For instance, a salesperson who will always have to complete her call reports.)**
  There are always going to be some activities that a person doesn't like doing. The question to ask is: Does she have to spend a *majority* of her time on these activities to deliver outstanding performance? If so, it might be time to suggest an alternative role. If not, what can she do differently to make the activities less draining, boring, or frustrating? Is there a way to shift perspective on the activity? Can she minimize the time she spends on it? Can she partner with a teammate? Going back and using the STOP interview can help you solve this problem.

- **What if your employee hasn't read this book, and can't describe vividly what his strengths and weaknesses are?**
  You need to arm yourself with a short list of questions that can elicit from the employee the information you need. I strongly recommend the following four. They won't reveal everything you may want to know about the employee's strengths and weaknesses, but they'll get you off on the right foot:
  - Where can I expect to see the best from you?
  - Where and when can I lean most heavily on you?

- When should I tread lightly with you?
- What kinds of situations should I actively steer you away from?

- **Find a forum where your people can share some of what they've learned about their strengths and weaknesses with their teammates.**

  Schedule time to sit down as a team and share your top three strengths and weaknesses with one another. Here's how this meeting might flow:

  1. Compile a spreadsheet of each person's top three strengths and weaknesses, and distribute it to the entire team.

  2. Ask each team member to pick his or her most dominant strength and describe it to the team.

  3. Then go around the room and ask each team member to give one example of when he or she has seen this strength in action. Here you are challenging the team to affirm one another.

  4. Repeat the previous two steps, but this time with each person's most draining weakness. And when you go around the room this time, be sure to ask each team member to describe if, and how he or she can help support the teammate's weakness.

  5. Consider: Are there certain activities you all love doing? If so, how can you sharpen and apply these strengths to help the team win and build its reputation? Are there situations that you should all put yourselves in; projects the team should volunteer for?

  6. Consider: Are there certain activities you all loathe doing? If there are, and you can't stop doing these activities, run them through the STOP interview. Maybe you can have a competition to see who can do this activity the quick-

est, and the winner gets a free lunch from the team. Or maybe you can take turns at this activity: One week Jon will do all the filing, the next week Margaret, and maybe the person who gets stuck with the filing that week gets a free specialty drink from Starbucks on "Filing Friday." Be creative on how you can reduce the amount of drag these activities exert on the team.

- **Be sure to use what you've learned about strengths and weakness when assigning roles and building project teams.** In theory, this appears complex, but in practice it often proves surprisingly straightforward. Since you've already laid the groundwork with steps one through four, and you've hopefully had productive one-on-one meetings with each team member, you'll find that when the time comes to discuss how the team can come together to attack a new project, your people will undoubtedly have lots of practical suggestions. Indeed, you may well find that building a strengths-based team proves as simple as this:

  1. As a team, sit down and determine project scope, goals, and outcomes.
  2. Ask the team to identify what specific tasks need to be done.
  3. Ask who is going to volunteer to do what.
  4. Anything left over? Lead a cleanup discussion about how the team members can partner with one another to make sure these remnants are taken care of.
  5. Optional: At your weekly meetings, ask all team members how much of their time they are spending playing to their strengths, and keep a running tally. This may seem a little gimmicky, but it's a good way to catch early whether one person is pulling the overall average down. The point

is not to cajole the person publicly, but to spur the team to swing into action and figure out how, together, they can help get this person, and hence the team, back on track.

Georgia, Heidi's manager, would be the first to admit that she is far from a perfect boss, but she nonetheless gives us a living, breathing example of many of these tips in action. In so doing, she reveals that it is possible to capitalize on each person's strengths despite the seismic marketplace shifts that so often change jobs dramatically or even sweep them aside.

In fact, as you'll see, Georgia's experience takes us one step further: she shows us that a great manager doesn't capitalize on people's strengths *despite* macro changes in the business world. Rather she deliberately *exploits* these changes in order to capitalize on each person's strengths more fully. Needless to say, this isn't always possible—sometimes dispassionate market forces eliminate jobs, and there's nothing a strengths-based manager can do about it. But what a strengths-based manager must always do is look for the opportunities hidden inside these forces. That's what Georgia did.

TEAM GEORGIA

At the same time that Heidi began the inward discipline of examining the activities that strengthen and weaken her at work, Georgia and her boss, Scott, began an outward look at where the hospitality industry was heading. It was clear to them that the hotel industry had turned around and was reversing out of a downward cycle. They saw it most vividly in the expansion of the Hampton brand, and they knew that this growth trend was going to affect not only Heidi but also the twelve other brand directors and the entire Hampton hotels Performance Support (HPS) team.

The evidence of this shift became glaringly obvious as she sat in a conference room at Hampton headquarters in Memphis. Georgia and the Hampton senior management team were discussing the annual budget for the coming year, and at the center of the table was a puzzle map of the United States. Each piece was tagged with the number of Hampton Inns located in that particular state. Next to that figure was the projected number of new hotels that were going to be built over the next three years. A quick glance at this 3-D model, and it was easy to see that there would be over one hundred new Hampton Inns peppering the country in the near future.

Georgia had only been in her role as a senior director of the Hampton Performance Support team for eight months, but her gut instinct as a manager kicked in. Immediately she began considering what this meant to her team and what actions she would have to take. Judging from the projected growth, she thought that one answer might be to add another region, which would mean hiring at least two new people. She briefly considered spreading the new hotels around to her current team members but quickly dismissed the notion, as she knew it would spread them too thin.

As she weighed her options, she became increasingly persuaded that this was an opportunity to shake things up and create a completely new structure for her division. "There wasn't anything wrong with the way we were doing things," says Georgia. "Our brand team always receives high satisfaction scores from our customers during our annual servey. But when you're looking at building one hundred new hotels per year over the next couple of years and are predicting that growth is going to continue, you have to think differently."

Now, it's important to point out that Georgia isn't the type of manager who feels it's necessary to stamp her reputation on the organization by creating massive upheaval. While Georgia was new to her role, she was not new to HPS. Before she was put in charge of the team, Georgia was a brand director just like Heidi and was therefore intimately aware of the repercussions that any change would have on her team.

Back in her office, Georgia focused on what it meant to be a brand director and thought about their wide variety of backgrounds. Each person had some kind of sales experience, and each had worked in the hospitality industry in some capacity. Some were former regional managers who had come up through Hampton hotels as either general managers or sales directors. Some used to work in quality assurance or on the operations side.

Perhaps it was unavoidable, but the brand-director role at Hampton reflected the diverse background of its directors and had evolved into a sort of jack-of-all-trades position within the hotel chain. Each brand director had more than one hundred hotels that she was supposed to support and, while each director tended to favor her previous area of expertise—sales and marketing, operations, or training—she was expected to be able to consult with her hotels on any and all issues that might come up.

At first glance, it would seem that Hampton's period of rapid growth would demand even more breadth from the team, since each would have more hotels requiring support. But what if the opposite were true? What if the brand directors went from being generalists to subject-matter experts? Would this enable each of them to deepen his contribution and therefore extend his capacity to help during this period of rapid growth? And if so, armed with this increased per-person capacity, would she be able to provide the necessary performance support to the hundreds of new hotels without adding a new director to the team?

Breaking the job down to its core components, Georgia detailed the key areas that her directors were primarily responsible for and determined that they fell into three main categories. First, brand directors had to consult with the hotels on the overall appearance of the facilities and how customers were treated. The rooms, the breakfast area, the front desk, they all had to be of a consistent standard throughout the chain.

Second, they looked for opportunities to improve the hotels' sales and revenue performance. They were charged with helping each hotel book rooms, whether by phone or online, making sure that hotels were aware of certain companywide special offers, and at the same time finding new ways to promote the overall image of the Hampton brand.

Finally, they were responsible for the opening of new hotels and the myriad things that had to be done—between the signing of the franchise agreements and the opening of the hotel—in order for a property to open its doors under the Hampton name.

Almost automatically, Georgia thought about her directors and considered what type of role each would want to play on a more specialized team. Was Heidi a sales and revenue person, or would she be more engaged working on new hotel openings? What about Tom? Georgia was pretty confident that he was a product and services guy. One by one, Georgia went through her list of directors and thought about where their strengths would best fit and where they would contribute the most to the team.

Soon thereafter, Georgia and Scott sat down to hash out how they could hone this notion into an actual structure. They discussed different ways to achieve Hampton's vision of becoming the number one franchiser in the midscale hotel segment. At the end of their conversation, they determined that perhaps the best way to get there was by reorganizing the division and separating the brand directors into three distinct category titles: director of sales and revenue, director of product and services, and director of new hotel openings.

After selling the plan to Phil, the senior VP of Hampton brand management, they started the process of assigning roles to directors.

They wondered how companies typically go about this kind of restructuring and asked their human resources team whether it was best to allow the directors to choose the role they wanted, or should Georgia assign roles according to her own evaluation? As is often the case in these situations, outside consultants were brought in, and the overall consensus was for Georgia to take the initiative and assign her team to the new director categories.

Georgia hesitated to follow their advice. "Just going in and saying 'This is what you're going to do' didn't feel like it was giving the new structure the best chance for success," says Georgia. "It just didn't feel right."

After a month of going back and forth with the consultants, Georgia decided to follow her own instincts. She scheduled a meeting with her team.

After Scott shared the new vision for the department and explained the strategic changes that brought it about, Georgia then presented the three new roles, listed the activities within each, and challenged her directors to identify which of the new roles would suit them best. She told them to spend a couple of days thinking about it and then schedule a one-on-one meeting with her to discuss their choice. Prior to their conversation, she gave them four questions to answer:

1. Which part of your job are you most passionate about?
2. Where have you had the greatest success in the last six months?
3. Where do you feel you could make your greatest contribution in the next one to three years?
4. Based on your strengths, talents, and abilities, where do you feel you can provide the most value on the brand team? (Each of the brand directors had not only captured, clarified, and confirmed his strengths, he had also taken the Myers-Briggs Type Indicator and the Clifton StrengthsFinder; Georgia asked them to consider their results when answering this question.)

Of course Georgia played out in her mind which role she thought each person would choose and even wrote down on paper what she thought the outcome would look like. "Most people aligned where I predicted," says Georgia, "but there were a couple of surprises."

Specifically, Irene. "I thought Irene was going to choose sales and revenue because that's what her background was," Georgia recalls, "but she chose new hotel openings instead. It wasn't until we sat down to discuss her decision that it really made sense to me." Apparently, to understand Irene, you needed to know one thing in particular about her: She didn't like not knowing what steps needed to be followed to do her job. And of all the positions, director of new hotel openings had the most clearly defined sequence of steps. New hotel owners had to be contacted according to a certain timetable, paperwork had to be filed by a certain deadline, and a preopening inspection had to be done by a specific date. And after the hotel opened, a postopening inspection had to be completed before the hotel could finally be turned over to a director of sales and revenue. Irene loved this kind of clarity.

"After our conversation, I thought back to prior team meetings and remembered how Irene was always the one that wanted to know the details and how Irene really doesn't like the unknown," says Georgia. "In retrospect, it made perfect sense for her to be in that role. But before we had our conversation, I had her down for something else."

While Georgia was open to changing her original idea about where she thought someone's strengths should be applied, in other instances she held her ground. "Tom came from an information technology and quality assurance background, and he has a strong understanding of the day-to-day mechanics of hotel operations," says Georgia. "I had him down for the director of product and services role. So when he told me that he wanted to be a director of sales and revenue, I was curious as to how he came to that conclusion." The first thing Georgia asked Tom was if he actually enjoyed sales calls. Taken slightly aback, and perhaps under the impression that he *should* enjoy sales calls, Tom maneuvered through an answer that concluded with "Doesn't everyone?"

Then Georgia asked what he typically focused on when he visited a hotel. Without hesitation, Tom immediately described how he likes to tour the property and look first at the rooms. He then said he loves nothing more than going through an improvement plan with the owner and detailing what needed to be done to bring all the various areas of the hotel into compliance with the franchise agreement. Last, he talked about the satisfaction he gets when helping an owner discover new ways to save money through various Hampton programs. "Every one of his answers screamed 'product and services' to me," Georgia says. "I think that as he listened to himself speak up about what he loved doing, even he became more aware of it. I don't think he walked away from that first conversation absolutely convinced that I'd put him in the right role, but in subsequent conversations, Tom has expressed how glad he is that I helped direct him to where his strengths are best expressed."

In the months since the new structure was announced, Georgia has already seen a dramatic increase in the entire team's performance.

"Now that they know where their focus is," says Georgia, "it's easier for them to see the specific results of their actions and what needs to be done to improve these results. For example, we have this Product Improvement Plan (PIP), which details what improvements a hotel needs to make in order to be in compliance with Hampton standards. The problem was that we had no central database to document where each hotel under a PIP stood in the process. Everyone was confused. Well, during a recent meeting, one of our product and services directors, Sheila, started talking about how PIPs could be improved. She had really good ideas and took the initiative and started working with the quality assurance team to build the database. At first the quality assurance folks said they might be able to have something up by the end of the year. But Sheila kept having conversations and explained how owners weren't able to understand what their expectations were, and how HPS wasn't able to make sure the owners had the resources to meet those expectations because they didn't know exactly where each hotel stood in the process."

Through these repeated talks, it soon became clear that the confusion caused by the lack of a database was translating into lost revenue and disenchanted franchise partners. The result? A system that was supposed to take eight months to create was up and running in two.

Another change that now seems obvious to Georgia but had never been done before was getting two of her directors of sales and revenue to attend the National Business Travel Association trade show. For the first time, Georgia's directors learned exactly what corporate clients like IBM, Home Depot, and GM expected in order for Hampton to be included in those companies' preferred business travel programs. "As a result, we had recently sent the IBM request for proposal for our hotels to be included in their preferred hotel program, and as a result of Karl's [one of the directors of sales marketing] attending the trade show he sent an email to his team explaining the importance of getting each of their hotels on board to understand what was necessary to attract corporate accounts," says Georgia. "I had never seen an email like that before from Karl. He was being totally proactive so that his hotels had another opportunity to generate revenue. Under the old structure, that never would have happened. Without a specific focus, brand directors were much more reactive."

And Heidi? As we mentioned in the previous step, Heidi, driven by her love of sharing ideas with willing owners and general managers, chose the director of new openings role. Now more focused than ever, she has made changes that are affecting not only Hampton but all of the Hilton brands. For example, in the past, because the process for setting up a database for a new hotel to be inputted in various booking channels could take two months or more to complete, new properties weren't instantly set up to take online reservations on the brand's website (or for that matter, any other website, such as Expedia and Travelocity). As a result, new hotels were delayed in their ability to begin accepting bookings in advance and secure revenue for dates when the property would be up and running.

That's now changing. Through conversations with Hampton's global data-management and e-business teams, Heidi has implemented a schedule of when hotels should be loaded into the system. This guarantees that new hotels will be up and on-line within thirty days of receipt of all required paperwork and well in advance of the hotel opening. "Last week I was copied on an email from a Hilton vice president to Phil saying that she was putting together a committee to look at new hotel opening processes and was looking for the best person from Hampton," says Georgia. "Well, that's Heidi's doing. She got the ball rolling on that and caused change for the whole of Hilton."

Talking from the conference room where it all started, Georgia points to the individual pictures of all her brand directors that line one of the walls. Ask her to name the strengths of any one person on her team, and she can easily list their three statements and recall insights she's discovered about them through one of the many conversations she's had about their strengths and weaknesses over the last few months.

Asked how the structural changes in her department have affected her job directly, she is quick to respond, "From a management standpoint, it's so helpful to have a clear understanding of who on my team will really be excited to do a particular project. Now, as soon as I learn of something that needs to be done, I think, 'That's a good project for Karl', or 'That's a good project for Heidi.' Knowing and sharing our strengths and weaknesses allows us to move so much faster, so much more efficiently. And once the projects are handed off to the right people, the ideas and initiative I'm seeing are miles ahead of where we were. When you get people in their strengths zone, their IQ seems to jump twenty points.

"The bottom line is we're getting a lot more done, and we're doing it better."

For a video challenge from me about Step 5, visit Simply Strengths.com.

BUILD STRONG HABITS

"HOW CAN YOU MAKE THIS LAST FOREVER?"

THE END OF THE BEGINNING

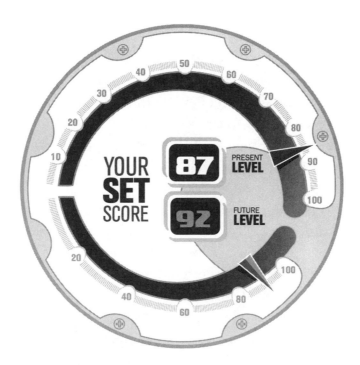

You first met Heidi back in step one. Now, six weeks later, this is her SET score. Talk to her, and you can hear the difference. Heidi's back. She's back to being what we all want to be at work: simultaneously effective and invigorated, able to get a lot done each week, yet still inquisitive, always looking for better ways of doing more. She's hungry again.

This transformation wasn't easy. She had to challenge her own entrenched beliefs, shift her focus away from some activities that appeared to be central to her job, and stick with this shift despite temptations to slip back into previous bad habits.

And it wasn't without risk. Like the time she confessed in front of Phil, the head of Hampton hotels, that she was no longer chasing hotels. Would he think she was trying to get out of work, that she was shirking her responsibilities? How should she explain to him that she was trying to contribute more, not less? Would he understand? At such times, she was certainly glad that her direct boss, Georgia, was embarking on the same journey. Georgia knew what she was going through.

In the end, though, Heidi made the transformation herself. She strapped on her own oxygen mask and did for herself what no one else could: She sorted through the jumble of activities that came down upon her each week and identified vividly her strengths and her weaknesses. She intentionally pushed her time at work toward the former and away from the latter, and, all the while, she managed to explain what she was doing persuasively enough to make those around her want to help. Her weeks at work now both reflect and require the best of her. She is living a strong life at work, and whether she stays in this job or moves on to others during her career, as she surely will, she sees no reason why this life can't last forever.

And there's no logical reason why it shouldn't.

Unfortunately, the world being what it is, there are many practical reasons why it won't.

She may get pulled back into the crazy, busy schedule that seems to afflict us all and neglect the discipline of pushing her world at work toward her strengths.

Or she may diligently devise a Strong Week Plan and stick to it successfully on Monday, Tuesday, and Wednesday. But come Thursday, she may start to get distracted, as people, problems, and one-off programs like the Hampton summits, press in upon her.

Or she may simply get discouraged. She may follow her Strong Week Plan and call upon her strengths each week as best she can—yet still not achieve her goals. This is hard. Often, when you miss a target or an expectation, you have the ready-made excuse that you didn't really have the chance to do what you do best; that you were put into a situation that didn't play to your strengths. But what if Heidi deliberately focused her time at work on activities that strengthened her and yet still failed to do what she set out to do? This is a far more bitter pill to swallow. Inevitably she may start to question whether her strengths are strong enough.

Or Georgia may move on, and Heidi may find herself managed by a boss who doesn't care as much about each person's distinct strengths and weaknesses.

Or she herself may move on. Having followed her Strong Week regimen for months on end, she may experience attention-getting success in her role and then be offered a different job, a bigger job, a bigger paycheck, a nicer office with a better view and a comfier chair—a job that, for all its benefits, may require her to be strengthened by the very activities that weaken her.

So yes, despite Heidi's stellar start in finding a path for her strengths, there are all manner of reasons why the hardest part will be staying on it.

And of course the same applies to you. By now you've done a lot of hard work. You've captured your strengths and weaknesses, made some tough decisions, had some tricky but hopefully productive conversations, and altered how and where you spend your time at work. You should now log onto Simply Strengths.com, retake the SET survey, and see how far you have progressed in capitalizing on your strengths over the past six weeks.

Obviously I don't know what your SET score is, but more than likely the needles have jumped to the right, and your attitude, your demeanor, and most important, your performance confirm it: Today you are playing to your strengths more consistently and more deliberately than you were six weeks ago.

Faced with a world that doesn't really care about your strengths, your challenge now is to continue and accelerate this progress by building strong habits. To help you, let's cut through the myriad things you could do and pinpoint the five things you absolutely must do to fight for this strong life of yours. It is, after all, your career, your professional life, your success, and satisfaction that is at stake.

THE STRONGEST HABITS

1. **Every day look over your three Strength Statements and your three Weakness Statements.**

   I realize that this sounds repetitive, but remember, what is powerful about these statements is their specificity. Since no one cares about your strengths and weaknesses as much as you do, and no one will take a stand for your strengths as resolutely as you will, it's up to you to fix them so clearly in your mind that you can recite them word for word from memory. When the blind will of the world tugs you back and forth, these specific statements will keep you clearheaded and show you how to stay productive, creative, and resilient. They will reinforce where you have made the greatest contribution and will point to where you will make even greater contributions in the future. So learn them; learn them by heart.

2. Every week complete a Strong Week Plan.

Start each week with a plan for making the week as close to an ideal week as possible. This means each week, identify two specific actions that you can take to leverage your strengths, and two actions to minimize your weaknesses. That's two ideas for each week, every week. Can't come up with any? Then pick one of your Strength Statements and run it through the FREE interview; or if it's a weakness, through the STOP interview. There is always room to maneuver within your job, and if you don't push to fill this room with activities that call upon the best of you, someone else will fill it with activities that don't. You've already begun the routine of the Strong Week Plan. Now you need to make it a habit; a habit that is stronger than the blind forces out there in the world.

3. Every quarter close the books on your strengths.

Put it on your calendar, once a quarter, to seek out your manager and have a thirty-minute conversation about your strong quarter. Look back over your Strong Week Plans and identify three highlights: three tangible achievements where you contributed more to the team based on either exploiting your strengths or minimizing your weaknesses. You will have done a lot in the last three months, and by the end of the quarter, much of it will have gotten lost in the blur. The point of this meeting is, first, to preserve in your mind and your manager's mind exactly where and how your strengths have helped. And second, to provide the raw material for where and how you can contribute more in the next quarter. You will benefit from this meeting—and whether your manager knows it or not, he will benefit as well. So push for it. Make him expect it.

4. Every six months pick a week and capture, clarify, and confirm your strengths.

Your underlying personality will not change much, but your strengths will. Capture these changes twice a year. After all, playing to your strengths does not mean only sticking to a small cluster of activities for your entire career. On the contrary, as your career progresses, you will surely stay inquisitive, and experiment, and volunteer for new responsibilities when the situation allows. And when you do, these new experiences may well cause some change in the specifics of your strengths and weaknesses.

Discipline yourself to keep on top of these subtle changes. Twice a year select a week and *capture* your emotional reaction to what you do during the week. Then, as you did in steps three and four, *clarify* your most dominant green and red pages. *Confirm* them with the Strength and Weakness Tests if you feel the need. Finally, write your three Strength Statements and your three Weakness Statements.

You may find that they remain exactly the same as before. In which case, going through the process will simply reinforce the need to pay heed to these particular strengths and weaknesses and build your life around them. Or, as I did, you may find that the specific content of both changes somewhat. Either way, if you are to maintain peak levels of performance and contribution throughout your career, it's up to you to keep track of how you're growing. Capturing, clarifying, and confirming twice a year will help.

5. Every year take the SET survey.

Most of us take things seriously only when we can measure them. Wealth, weight, speed, fuel consumption, everything, becomes so much more interesting to us when we can measure it with a simple metric. Tell us to stop eating butter, and we'll ignore you. Tell us that our bad cholesterol is over 200, and we snap to attention. The same applies to putting your strengths to work. Unless you stamp a number on it, it won't grab your attention, and without your full attention, you will be vulnerable to the push-pull of your working world. So take the SET survey each year. You'll see movement, and this movement will serve as a leading indicator of your performance and contribution. Pay attention to it. It will show you your future.

Even if you implement these five strong habits with passion and rigor, you will inevitably face a few situations that will slow or even halt your progress. To prepare you to survive them with your strengths focus intact, here are nine of the most common. You may not experience all of them in your career, but the chances are you'll come up against at least half of them.

"AND WHAT HAPPENS IF . . ."

1. ". . . I don't know if I should take this job?"
   Whenever you are considering a new role, the three questions most people ask themselves are, first, "What is the fundamental purpose of the role, and do I have an appetite for this purpose?" For example, do you have a fascination for the fundamental purpose of journalism, or advertising, or health care? A role whose purpose leaves you cold will more than likely not be a good fit.
   Second, "What are the kinds of people I'll be working with?" Since you'll obviously be more productive if you forge strong relationships with your colleagues, you need to meet some of these people before you decide to take the job and,

five strong habits

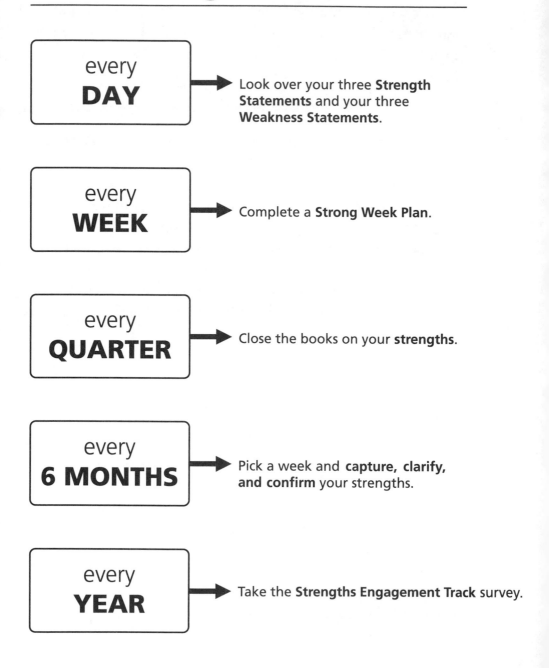

every
DAY

→ Look over your three **Strength Statements** and your three **Weakness Statements**.

every
WEEK

→ Complete a **Strong Week Plan**.

every
QUARTER

→ Close the books on your **strengths**.

every
6 MONTHS

→ Pick a week and **capture, clarify, and confirm** your strengths.

every
YEAR

→ Take the **Strengths Engagement Track** survey.

as far as you can, judge whether they share your values, your sense of humor, and your interests.

And third, "What are the specific activities that will fill my week?" The job title may say "customer support specialist," but what this actually means is dealing with angry customers all day long. Do you like this kind of confrontation? Likewise, the job title may say "financial consultant," but what this translates to is trying to persuade people to invest money with your institution. Do you like asking people for money?

These three questions are quite straightforward, but what most people forget is that, of the three, by far the most important is the last one. "What are the specific activities that will fill my week?" No matter how much you resonate with the purpose of the role or how much you bond with your future colleagues, it is the activities themselves that will determine your success. The activities always trump the purpose and the people. The "what" always trumps the "why" and the "who with."

It's not that the "why" and the "who with" are unimportant. For example, deciding to get into nursing because you yearn to take care of sick people is sound thinking. Likewise, wanting to join the emergency room team because you jell with the people on the team is equally sound.

It's just that the "what" is more important. If your strengths lie in the activity of building long-term relationships with patients, and in tweaking different therapies according to ongoing feedback from a patient, your typical day in the ER will not give you the chance to use these strengths. Instead it will actively prevent them. You'll walk in each day and find that the patients you saw yesterday have disappeared either into a regular ward or back out into the world.

And so, over time, your frustrations will rise, and your contributions to the ER team will diminish.

Faced with these frustrations, you may turn for inspiration to your strong sense of mission for helping the sick, but this mission will not restore you. Or you may turn to your strong relationships with your colleagues on the team, but they will not sustain you. You are looking in the wrong place. Your problem is that the activities that fill up your minutes at work are the wrong ones for you. They don't call upon your strengths.

So before you decide whether to take this new role, push for specifics. What will a Monday look like? A Tuesday? Can you talk to one of the best in the role to find out? Don't make your decision until you have.

And once you've identified what the activities are, mull them over for a day or two. Imagine yourself doing them . . . and then getting up the next morning and doing them again. Don't look past them to the title you'll be getting or, worse yet, to the next job—the job that you were promised in a few months "if all goes well with this job." Taking a job whose activities drag you down simply because you are enticed by the job that might come afterward is a gamble. More often than not, the actual job drags you down to such an extent that there is no next job, or when it comes, your reputation is sullied.

The best reason to take a job is always that the activities of the job itself intrigue you and strengthen you.

2. ". . . I don't think I should have taken this job."
So you took the job, but something went awry in your discovery process or your decision-making process. Or perhaps

you were misled or circumstances changed. Anyway, you're in the job, a couple of months have gone by, and now you're certain that you've taken a wrong turn. Why couldn't you have seen that this would happen? How could you have been so blind? You're kicking yourself.

Well, fine, heed your emotions, but don't beat yourself up too badly. Since the working world is dynamic, and human beings are complex creatures, most people experience a misstep at one point or another during their career. However, what you must do is face up to it fast and take action to get yourself out of it. Occasionally this will mean packing up and leaving the role, but more often than not, you'll be able to track your way back onto your strengths path without resorting to something quite as drastic.

Kellie Barton is now the head of leadership development at Franciscan Missionaries of Our Lady Health System, which serves three hundred thousand patients in and around Baton Rouge, Louisiana (though since Hurricane Katrina hit in 2005 that number has jumped significantly). But eight years ago, she was the new human resources specialist, having just transferred over from a smaller local hospital. She made the move because she'd been assured that she would be given the chance to build relationships with lots of different people throughout the system and then devise training programs and on-the-job experiences to help these people learn and grow—two strengths of hers.

But what the job turned out to be was an order taker.

"We need sixty nurses by next Wednesday."

"We need forty new technicians right away."

Kellie found herself on the phone 90 percent of the time, interviewing one candidate after another, making a spot decision to hire or not, and then passing the person down the production line to orientation and training, so that she could then jump back on the phone and get the process started with another candidate. And she hated it. There was no opportunity to build a relationship with anyone, no chance to help anyone get better at something. "It was awful," she says now. "Every day I felt like a cat whose fur was being deliberately rubbed backward. In fact, I've kept my calendar from this time so that I have a reminder to never, ever go back to this kind of job again."

Did she quit? No, she had a tough but clear conversation with her boss. She said, "This isn't working for me. I know you told me to stick this out for six months, and then I would get to develop people, but I can't. I know my numbers look great, I've filled all my openings on time, but it's turning me into a bad employee, a bad wife and mother. I want to—really need to—go develop people and programs."

Rather than ushering her sternly out of the office, her boss surprised her by announcing that, as it happened, Our Lady of the Lake was in the early stages of developing its leadership development program, and that Kellie would probably be a good person to take on the project. Which she did. And still does.

In recounting this story, Kellie calls this a "wonderful coincidence," but is it really?

"Coincidences" such as this often happen when someone identifies a specific strength, takes a stand for this strength, and volunteers it to her team. If ever you find yourself in a situation where you are convinced that you've taken the wrong job, volunteer a specific strength of yours and see if you encounter a similar coincidence.

3. "... I'm new to the job."

This is always a little disorienting. You are new to the role, so you don't know the people, the technical elements of the job, and, most importantly, you don't know the unwritten rules: who really makes the decisions, who needs to know everything, who should never be bothered unless the building's collapsing. What should you do? What is the best strategy to make a bold first move and be immediately productive while still getting your bearings?

Simply put, you should pick a strength and rely on it. That's what Kellie did when given her new assignment. She didn't really know what kind of programs she should design, who exactly she should design them for, or even whether anybody in the hospitals actually wanted leadership development programs. Faced with this ambiguity, she fell back on one of the few things she was certain of: namely, that she was at her best when sitting in someone else's office or some other facility's cafeteria, chatting to people about what was on their minds at work, putting faces to voices, and starting to build relationships. In her words, "I just went out and met people. It's what I knew how to do. So I did it."

You should do the same. Pick one of your strengths and lead with it. When all else is uncertain, this strength of yours will not only showcase you in the most self-assured and confident light possible, it will also provide a core of certainty, a sure beachhead from which you can start reaching out and filling in the gaps in your knowledge.

4. "... I'm constantly overworked."

You're not going to fix this problem overnight. It took you a while to become overworked, so it will take you a while to get out from under it. Start by picking one of your frenetic weeks and capture the greens and the reds of the week. As you did before, select your three most dominant greens. Then, rather than turning your top three greens into Strength Statements, simply set them up on your desk and commit yourself to making them a priority for an entire month. As far as you can, push your time at work toward them. Tell yourself that anything that is not one of those three activities will be relegated to your "ask only" pile: namely, it gets done only if someone asks you for it. For a full month, no more volunteering for projects because they seem interesting, because they'll make someone else happy, or because they'll lead to experiences that could help your career sometime in the future. Concentrate on your three strongest greens and push everything else aside.

See what happens after a month. You may find that an awful lot of stuff falls by the wayside, leaving you to concentrate on what you do best.

Of course, you may find that people repeatedly ask you to do some of the things that turned up in your red pile or were lower down on your green pile. In which case, the best fallback position is to figure out a system that can contain these activities and limit the amount of time you have to spend on them.

Kathy Twells, a vice president of area sales for Coca-Cola, has introduced something called "Skip Level Day" so that she can accommodate the many people, from all different levels of the company, who want to come to her for career advice.

Kellie Barton has a wackier system to solve pretty much the same problem. On a day when she needs uninterrupted time to flesh out an idea into a full-fledged program, or to complete a complex report, she wears her Zone Socks. These are obnoxious lime green and orange socks, which she flashes boldly when she arrives in the morning, and which her team now knows means that she is not to be disturbed during the day. "One day," she says, "I wore them as a joke because I had to think differently that day. So I told everyone that I was dressing differently in order to get my mind in the proper gear. Everyone sort of laughed, but ever since then, they know that if I've got the Zone Socks on, they should stay out of my office. It's great because I'm terrible at turning people away."

5. ". . . my manager doesn't understand me."
This is going to happen a lot. Not because the world is full of managers who don't listen well—although many don't—but because no manager, no matter how perceptive and empathic, is ever going to understand the quintessence of you. No manager will ever be able to see the world through your eyes. No one will ever truly understand why you hate surprises the way you do, or why you just can't stand to lose, or why you can stand to lose to *this* person under *this* set of circumstances, but not to *that* person, never, under any circumstances, to *that* person. Or why your mind soars with ideas and spirit whenever you are trying to persuade a group of skeptical clients, but it shuts down when you see the same skeptical look on your manager's face. You feel these subtle reactions as forcefully as a punch, but no one else does or ever will. To everyone else, you are, on some level, unfathomable.

So if you find yourself thinking "My manager just doesn't understand me," the best advice is to get over it. She'll *never* truly understand you. The burden falls on you to understand yourself in as much detail as possible, so that you can then go to her and describe vividly which activities and situations will draw the best out of you, and which won't. As you saw in step five, it's her responsibility to be open to ways to maximize your strengths and minimize your weaknesses. If she doesn't, you may want to consider moving on. But it will always be your responsibility to supply her with the raw material.

6. ". . . my manager is an idiot."

Your manager probably isn't an idiot. He just doesn't have the same strengths as you, and so, from your perspective, he keeps doing things that are wrongheaded and that are losing your department the respect within the organization. So while he may not be an idiot, he is in your view a problem. He's frustrating your strength, and he's hurting the department.

Faced with this situation, you always have the option of seeking out a role in a different department or leaving the organization entirely.

But before you jump—and remember, your frying pan may be hot, but fire's hotter, and there's a lot of dry brush out there—try this: Identify the exact strength that he's frustrating, and then deliberately seek out one small situation this week where this strength can prove useful to one of your department's clients. Whether the client is internal or external doesn't matter, it just has to be a situation where a client will benefit. Apply your strength to this situation and really push yourself to apply it as well as you can so that you feel that thrill again, that no-other-feeling-quite-like-it of your strength in action. Then do it again next week and the week after.

This will certainly solve your frustration. It will also serve to polish your department's reputation. These small successes will gain your department external supporters and give these supporters stories to tell about you and your colleagues.

This is precisely what was done by Clive Spencer (a pseudonym). Clive worked for a high-tech company in the strategic planning department. He was a brilliant strategic thinker, with a mind that could play out in vivid detail one possible scenario after another and select the most advantageous. His problem was that his boss didn't have a strategic bone in her body. Despite heading up the strategic planning department, her strengths lay far more toward the planning end of the spectrum.

After months of growing frustration, rather than quitting, Clive decided to seek out one small situation where he could flex his strategic strength. Another group within the company was having trouble deciding among various possible product mixes for the Asian market, and it had turned to Clive's group for help. Distracted by his intense frustrations, he had put the request on a mental back burner. Now he focused in on it. He called a three-day off site with their group, which he designed and led, and helped them make their selection for the product mixes. Over the next few months, he stayed close to the project as the Asian team tweaked its mixes according to feedback from the marketplace.

The results indicated success all around. Clive exploited his strength, experienced some success, bolstered the reputation of his department, and showed his boss what strategic thinking actually looked like.

Well, not *quite* all around. Clive's boss is still strategically impaired, and he still can't quite believe that such a person should be running the strategic planning department. And he's probably right. But that's life. You can whine about it, or you can give of your best where you have the best to give, and reap the rewards of this excellence. Clive chose this approach. He chose to flourish. You should too.

7. "... I'm burned out."

Burnout doesn't happen when you are working long hours on invigorating activities. Long hours may tire you out, but they rarely burn you out. But fill your weeks with the wrong kinds of activities, activities that weaken you, and even regular hours will start the burn.

Unfortunately, most of us will have to contend with this. Whether you like variety and so are constantly looking for new responsibilities, or you are successful and keep getting promoted, or you are responsible and always attentive to the pressures of this person's needs and that person's expectations and this new program and that new priority, it is highly likely that at some point in your career your weeks will start to fill up with weakening activities. You may not notice this immediately, not only because you are busy and focused on getting the job done, but because these shifts in how you spend your time at work are subtle and incremental. It's only after months have gone by that you wake up one day and realize that you are squeezing the life out of the steering wheel to and from work. In this sense, burnout happens like bankruptcy does: at first, gradually, then suddenly.

This was Heidi's predicament, of course. She wasn't in the wrong job. She was in the right job, doing the wrong things.

And her path to a solution should be your path. Pick a week; capture, clarify, and confirm which activities strengthen and which weaken; then start the week-by-week process of pushing your time toward the former and away from the latter.

8. "... in the grand scheme of things, my job's just not that important."
Some people struggle to become one of the two out of ten who play to their strengths because, on some level, they don't appreciate their strengths. In fact, if given the choice, they would like to have different strengths. I see this played out often when people tell me their Clifton StrengthsFinder results. Although each theme description was written positively, it's clear that some themes are deemed much more desirable than others. For example, the theme Strategic is very popular, as are Developer, Individualization, and Futuristic. In contrast, the people who see Woo or Significance or Adaptability on their profile are the ones who tend to sidle up to me and ask whether it's possible to change their results by retaking the profile.

You can't blame people for doing this. In many subtle and not-so-subtle ways, society tells us what's valuable and what's not—for example, that being strategic and future focused are tickets to the executive suite, whereas being a good wooer and craving significance for yourself get you not much of anything.

To make your greatest possible contribution, however, you're going to have to look beyond society's judgments. And here I'll refer you back to Warren Buffett. He knows as well as anybody that while society thinks that being a smart business person is admirable, it reserves its greatest admiration for the smart businessman who selflessly yearns to make the world a better place. He could have just handed the money over to Bill Gates and said, "He can give it away better than me."

But Buffett couldn't leave it at that. Something compelled him to go on and say, "Besides, philanthropy isn't fun for me." At the time, many commentators took this as yet another sign of his self-deprecating Midwestern humility. But I think the opposite is true. I think he's proud of his strengths. He's proud that he's fascinated by margins; proud that he's intrigued by analyzing the fundamentals of a business; proud that when it comes to the equations of business, he trusts his judgment. Proud too that each of these invigorates him in a way that the activities of philanthropy never could.

I'm not at all suggesting he's arrogant, merely that he is deeply comfortable with his own particular strengths. He realizes that his strengths lead him to make a certain kind of contribution, and he's proud to tell the world that he wants to keep making it.

We could all do with taking this page out of Buffett's book and applying it to our own strengths. In the moral universe, some activities are obviously weightier than others. A good friend of mine is a pediatric cardiologist specializing in infant open-heart surgery. I'm a business researcher and consultant. There's no question her work is more important to the world than mine. But so what? What can I do about that? I suppose I could bemoan the fact that I was horrible at biology in school, am inept with any implement in my hands, and never wanted to be a doctor. But what a waste of my time and energy that would be.

Likewise, you may be a concrete thinker who, like Clive Spencer's boss, prefers tactical real-world planning, but who deep down wishes that you could be as intrigued by strategic theorizing as some of your colleagues are. But, again, what a waste of time. Strategic theorizing will never engage you, in the same way that philanthropy will never engage Buffet.

All any of us can do is know ourselves well enough to identify where our greatest possible contributions lie, and then do our utmost to make those contributions real.

9. "... deep down, I don't think I'm as good as everyone says I am."

Have you ever had this feeling? This feeling that maybe you are not quite as good as everybody says you are, that maybe if they turned on all the lights in all the corners, they would find you out? Many of us have experienced this feeling—so many of us, in fact, that there is a name for it: imposter syndrome. And, unfortunately, on some level you are right to have these feelings. Unless you're Tiger Woods or Bill Gates or Warren Buffett, the chances are that there is indeed someone out there who is better than you at selling, or finding patterns in data, or making presentations, or writing books, or whatever your job is.

But what of it? You can't control how good someone else is, and you can't control what anyone else thinks of you. All you can control is how you choose to spend your time at work. And you now know the discipline of how to spend that time wisely. You know how a strength feels and how a weakness feels. You know how to push your time at work toward your strengths and away from your weaknesses. You know how to talk about your strengths without boasting and your weaknesses without whining. And you know what you need to do to keep capitalizing on your strengths despite the pressures of the world at large.

So whenever you hear that sly, small voice whispering

"Maybe you're not that good. Maybe you don't really know what you're doing," look back to this new discipline and take confidence in it. This discipline is all you need to make your greatest possible contribution for the longest possible period of time.

Of course, even with this discipline, standing up for your strengths will never be without risk. The French writer Anaïs Nin had a nice line on risk. I'm sure she wasn't referring to strengths, but nonetheless it serves us well: *"And the day came when the risk it took to remain tight in the bud became more painful than the risk it took to blossom."*

I hope this book has brought this day closer. Yes, there are risks to blossoming; there are risks to betting your life on your strengths, but for you, from this day forward, the risks of not doing so are far greater.

For a video challenge from me about Step 6, visit Simply Strengths.com.

CODA: TAKE YOUR STAND

This is what I believe:

I believe that you have distinct strengths.

I believe that no one has quite the same configuration of strengths as you.

I believe that you will be at your most productive, creative, focused, generous, and resilient when you figure out how to play to your strengths most of the time.

And I believe that when you do, your customers, your colleagues, your company, and you will win. Everyone will win.

But in the end, it doesn't much matter what I believe. It matters only what you believe.

So let tomorrow be a different day than today. Let tomorrow be a stronger day than today. Let tomorrow begin with your asking yourself "What are my strengths, and how can I contribute them today?" and let every day thereafter begin the same way. You've always known what your strengths are. You've always known what lies within you. So trust your strengths, be proud of them, and take your stand.

ACKNOWLEDGMENTS

Judi, whether you knew it or not at the time, you started this book. It is my best attempt to capture the spirit and the practice of what you strive for every day. Thank you for being the example.

Kevin, you are all over this book. Without your guidance, your energy, and your good judgment, it would have been a much smaller and humbler work. Thank you for always showing me the right way forward.

Charlotte, as you know, there are sections of this book that reflect the fine distinctions of your thinking. The entire book reflects your good heart.

Jayme, designer, marketer, sometime whale rider, we all miss you.

Maggie, you, of all people, are on the vanguard of the strengths movement. You have developed a world-class expertise ridiculously quickly, and so you, of all people, must be the judge of this book.

Alison, I wish you lived just around the corner.

Rebecca, thank you for your designs, your inquisitiveness, and if you'll allow, your inspiration over the last nine months.

Mike, I am not entirely sure how you do what you do, but I thank the universe every day that you can.

Vicki and Jen, you may not recognize yourselves in this book, but your spirit and your ideas informed much of it. Thank you for knowing so early that we were all on the right path.

Trombone Player Wanted is the film-of-the-book. It began as a vague yearning to accelerate the strengths movement through video. And things would have stayed vague were it not for the talents of a few wonderful people. At Dutchville, Sonny, Rene, and Brett. At Best Buy, Bill and his team. And the through-line of it all, Tom. Thank you for raising it up.

Among my clients: Tim and Andy, Phil and Gina, Cheryl and Stuart, Steve and Stacey, Traci and Rena, thank you for your expectations of us, and above all, your belief. Heidi and Georgia, thank you for your willingness to trust us.

Among my old friends: Courtney and Denison, how great to march into the fray with you both after so long. Martha, Dominick, Suzanne, Carisa, and the incomparable Wylie: thank you for your confidence and for never settling. Joni, I love you and miss you. And Fred, you know how I feel about our partnership. This book bears your stamp as clearly as do all the others.

Among my new friends: Jennifer. Talk about strength. I think we all feel a little more invigorated and more resilient knowing you're around.

Mom and Dad, Neil and Pips, Linda and Mitch, I love you.

Mark, how fun was this, huh? Thank you for the stories, the sass, and the existential chats.

Em, another helter-skelter year together. You are quite simply the best at what you do. And Olive—yes, you, Olive. You are too.

Janie, Jack, Lilia: hang on tightly to one another. There's strength in numbers.

ABOUT THE AUTHOR

MARCUS BUCKINGHAM spent seventeen years at the Gallup Organization, where he conducted research into the world's best leaders, managers, and workplaces. The Gallup research later became the basis for the bestselling books *First, Break All the Rules* and *Now, Discover Your Strengths,* both coauthored by Buckingham. Buckingham has been the subject of in-depth profiles in *The New York Times, Fortune, BusinessWeek,* and *Fast Company.* He now has his own company, providing strengths-based consulting, training, and e-learning. He lives in Southern California with his wife, Jane, and their two children, Jackson and Lilia.

RESOURCE GUIDE

How Engaged Are Your Strengths?

The Strengths Engagement Track™ (SET).
SET is a metric designed to measure exactly how engaged your strengths are at work.

INDIVIDUAL: How to get your own Strengths Engagement Track™ (SET) Score.
Your SET score provides you a real time comparison of how engaged your strengths are as compared to the rest of the working world.

To Take The Strengths Engagement Track™ (SET):
- Retrieve the Strengths Engagement Track™ ID code from the reverse side of the back jacket of this book.
- Go to http://www.simplystrengths.com. Follow the instructions to take the SET survey. You will be presented with a screen to input your SET ID code.
- Complete the SET survey.
- You will receive your Individual SET report at the conclusion of the survey.

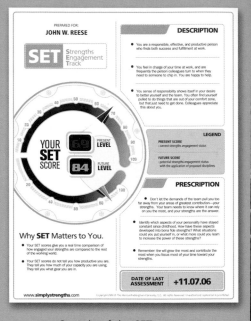

Sample of the SET report

TEAM: How to link multiple SET scores together to reveal how engaged the entire team's strengths are.
If you are a manager, you should have your entire team take the SET survey to see how much of your team's strengths potential is being used.

To Administer The SET Survey For Your Team:
- Upon completion of your Individual SET, you will have the option of inviting your team to complete a Team SET survey.
- To set up your Team, e-mail invitations to your team members.
- Provide a copy of the book, *Go Put Your Strengths To Work*, to each team member.
- After each individual has retrieved their own ID code from the reverse side of the back jacket of the book, have them go to http://www.simplystrengths.com to take the SET survey. Your Team members will reference your iD code to be tied to the same team.
- You will receive an email alert to view your team's participation of the SET survey. When you feel enough team members have completed the SET survey, you may run the Team SET report.

Download The Short Film Series

Trombone Player Wanted
To help you bring the strengths movement to life we offer you a compelling short film series that follows the same 6 step discipline as the book. Each of the 6 short films in *Trombone Player Wanted* lasts between 10-15 minutes. They tell the story of an eight year old boy, Ewan, and his struggles to take a stand for his strengths and put them to work.

How Do I Download The Short Films?
Your purchase of the book, *Go Put Your Strengths To Work*, gave you the right to one free download of the first two short films in the *Trombone Player Wanted* series. Watch them online (stream) or simply download them for viewing later.

To Access The First Two Films:
- Visit http://www.simplystrengths.com.
- Input your ID code (which is found on the inside dust jacket of the book).
- Choose to either stream the short film or download to view them later.

How Does This Short Film Series Work For You?
We live in a world where video can be accessed at faster and faster speeds and can be played on everything from cell phones and iPods to sixty inch HD plasma screens. *Trombone Player Wanted* is designed to capitalize on the power of video and help you spread the word about the strengths movement.

Use The Discussion Questions

It Begins With You
We wrote *Trombone Player Wanted* for you.

You may want to show it to your team right away, but please don't. As the airlines are fond of saying "Put your own oxygen mask on first before you start trying to help those around you." Yes, your team will benefit from finding their strengths and putting them to work, but you will only be a hindrance if you don't know how to do this with your strengths in your life.

So watch each of the films on your own before you share it.

Watch. Discuss. Apply.
The experience of *Trombone Player Wanted* consists of more than just plugging in your DVD and watching a short film. Some of the ideas in the films are not commonly held. Some of them are commonly held but rarely applied. The films should bring these ideas to the surface and stimulate some personal reflection, and public discussion.

To help you, the following pages are filled with questions. Some are personal. Others are meant to start a discussion within your team.

To maximize the *Trombone Player Wanted* experience:

- Download and watch *Trombone Player Wanted* Step 1

- Review the discussion questions for Step 1, first individually and then with your team

- Download and watch *Trombone Player Wanted* Step 2

- Repeat the process by reviewing the discussion questions for Step 2, first individually and then with your team

STEP 1
SO, WHAT'S STOPPING YOU?

Think back to when you were a child.

Can you see any positive patterns of behavior that have stayed with you since as far back as you can remember?

How have they developed over the years?

How do you channel and focus these strengths today?

Do you find yourself dwelling on your weaknesses a lot?

How does it make you feel?

Why do you do it?

Who asks you to?

Do you think you should?

Do you know any people who are passionate about what they do and who seem to spend a lot of time doing activities that they love?

Find the time to talk with two of them.

How often do they get to play to their strengths?

How did they make this happen?.

Do they ever find it difficult to stay on their strengths path?

Did they ever find themselves straying from this path?

How did they get back on?

STEP 2
DO YOU KNOW WHAT YOUR STRENGTHS ARE?

Which specific activities did you find yourself looking forward to last week?

Do you always seem to look forward to these activities?

Why?

Was there any time last week when you got in your zone?

And you found it easy to concentrate?

And time just flew by?

What were you doing?

Look back for all these telltale signs of a strength.

Can you see anything?

Which specific activities last week made you feel strong?

Are your strengths central to your week at work?

Trombone Player Wanted Facilitator Kit

Do you want to lead your team through the *Trombone Player Wanted* short film series but need a little help?

The *Trombone Player Wanted* Facilitator Kit provides you with the tools you need to lead others through the six step experience including:

A Facilitator's Guide containing a step-by-step description of how to use the films in a classroom setting.

A DVD-ROM containing Power Point slides for facilitation, documents that help you set up and introduce participants to the program, and participant guides that you can customize, print and distribute.

A single copy of *Go Put Your Strengths To Work* by Marcus Buckingham.

20 copies of the short film series *Trombone Player Wanted* for class participants.

For more information on the *Trombone Player Wanted* Facilitator Kit visit www.SimplyStrengths.com.

Become a Strengths-based Organization

Your Case Study

Imagine that you are a senior leader of a large retail chain. Below is a chart plotting your stores by profit and local economic potential. The question that keeps bothering you when you look at this graph is why is there so much range in the performance of your stores. It is especially concerning that two stores that have the same economic potential (see arrows) can vary so significantly in profit performance. In each store the same kinds of employees sell the same kinds of products to the same kinds of customers in the same kinds of neighborhoods, and one store massively outperforms the other one. Why? What is causing this range? What is going on in the teams at the top that isn't going on in the teams at the bottom?

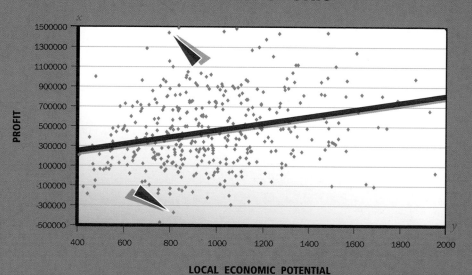

At The Marcus Buckingham Company we are consumed with answering this question.

If you are interested in learning how to build high performing teams please visit www.SimplyStrengths.com and download Marcus Buckingham's free white paper.

Capture Your Activities

Introduction To The reMEMO™

In Step Two of *Go Put Your Strengths to Work*, you are presented with a three phase process to help you identify your strengths. The first phase requires you to capture which specific activities over the course of a week played to your strengths and which ones played to your weaknesses.

To help you capture these activities, the next section contains sixteen green and sixteen red reMEMO™ pages from a learning tool we use called a reMEMO™ pad.

- Each day over the next week record specific activities that you *Loved* on the green reMEMO™ pages and specific activities that you *Loathed* on the red reMEMO™ pages.
- You should only write one activity per page.
- There are probably activities that you don't love or loathe. These are neutral zone activities. Don't worry about capturing these. Simply focus on those activities that you really love or loathe.

At the end of the week, you'll be tearing out the pages you've written on. Refer back to Step Two of the book for detailed instructions on how to use what you've captured to drill down on your Strengths and Weaknesses.

Sample reMEMO™ pages:

I *Loved* It   reMEMO™

I felt strong when...

I renegotiated a contract with Brad Coleman's company for another four years.

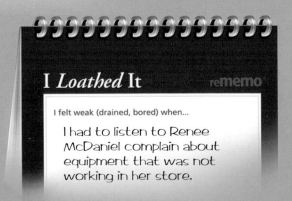

I *Loathed* It   reMEMO™

I felt weak (drained, bored) when...

I had to listen to Renee McDaniel complain about equipment that was not working in her store.

I *Loved* It

I felt strong when...

I *Loved* It

I felt strong when...

I *Loved* It

I felt strong when...

I *Loved* It

I felt strong when...

I *Loved* It

I felt strong when...

I *Loved* It

rememo

I felt strong when...

I *Loved* It

I felt strong when...

I *Loved* It

I felt strong when...

I *Loved* It

I felt strong when...

I *Loved* It

I felt strong when...

I *Loved* It

I felt strong when...

I *Loved* It

I felt strong when...

I *Loved* It

I felt strong when...

I *Loved* It

I felt strong when...

I *Loved* It

I felt strong when...

I *Loved* It

I felt strong when...

I *Loathed* It

I felt weak (drained, bored) when...

I *Loathed* It

I felt weak (drained, bored) when...

I *Loathed* It

I felt weak (drained, bored) when…

I *Loathed* It

I felt weak (drained, bored) when…

I *Loathed* It

I felt weak (drained, bored) when...

I *Loathed* It

I felt weak (drained, bored) when...

I *Loathed* It

I felt weak (drained, bored) when...

I *Loathed* It

I felt weak (drained, bored) when...

I *Loathed* It

I felt weak (drained, bored) when...

I *Loathed* It

I felt weak (drained, bored) when...

I *Loathed* It

I felt weak (drained, bored) when...

I *Loathed* It

I felt weak (drained, bored) when...

I *Loathed* It

I felt weak (drained, bored) when…

I *Loathed* It

I felt weak (drained, bored) when…

I *Loathed* It

I felt weak (drained, bored) when...

I *Loathed* It

I felt weak (drained, bored) when...